FOR ORGANS, PIANOS & ELECTRONIC KEYBOARDS

E Z PLAY TODAY

36

GOOD OL' SONGS
66 TREASURED FAVORITES

ISBN 0-634-01835-3

HAL•LEONARD®
CORPORATION
7777 W. BLUEMOUND RD. P.O. BOX 13819 Milwaukee, WI 53213

Visit Hal Leonard Online at
www.halleonard.com

CONTENTS

Aba Daba Honeymoon

Registration 4
Rhythm: Fox Trot or March

Words and Music by Arthur Fields
and Walter Donovan

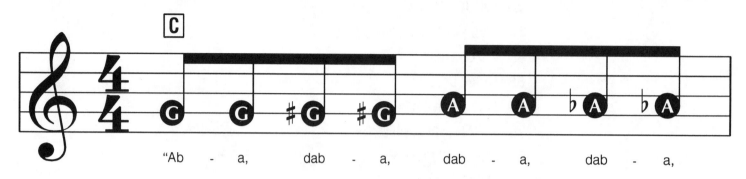

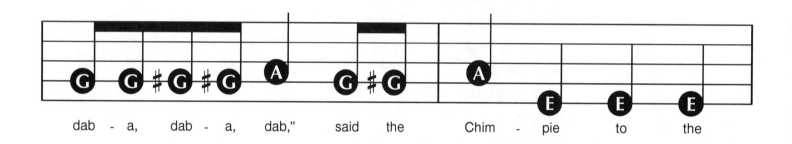

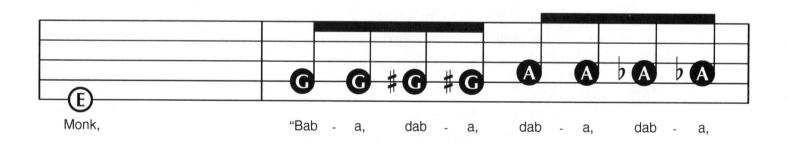

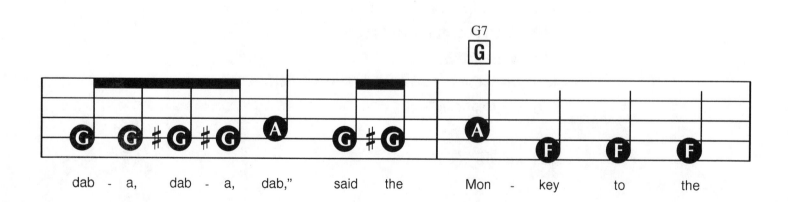

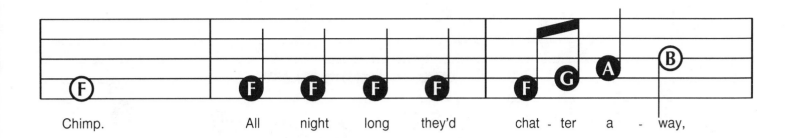

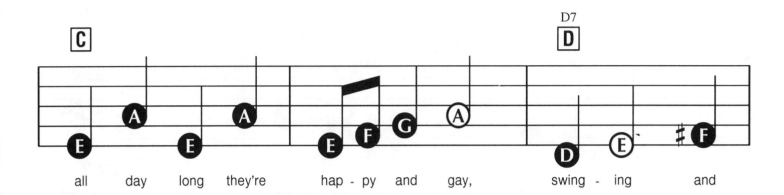

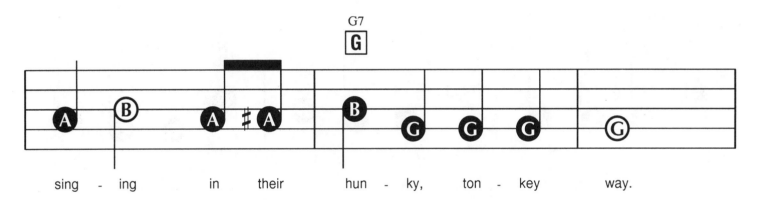

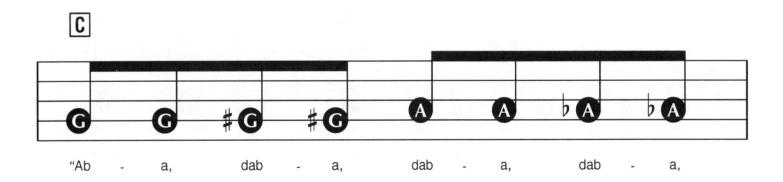

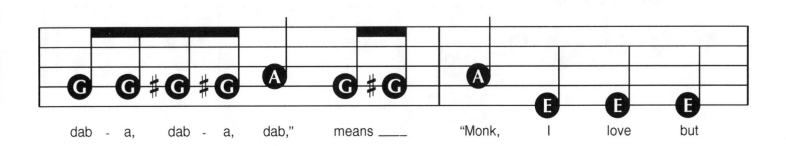

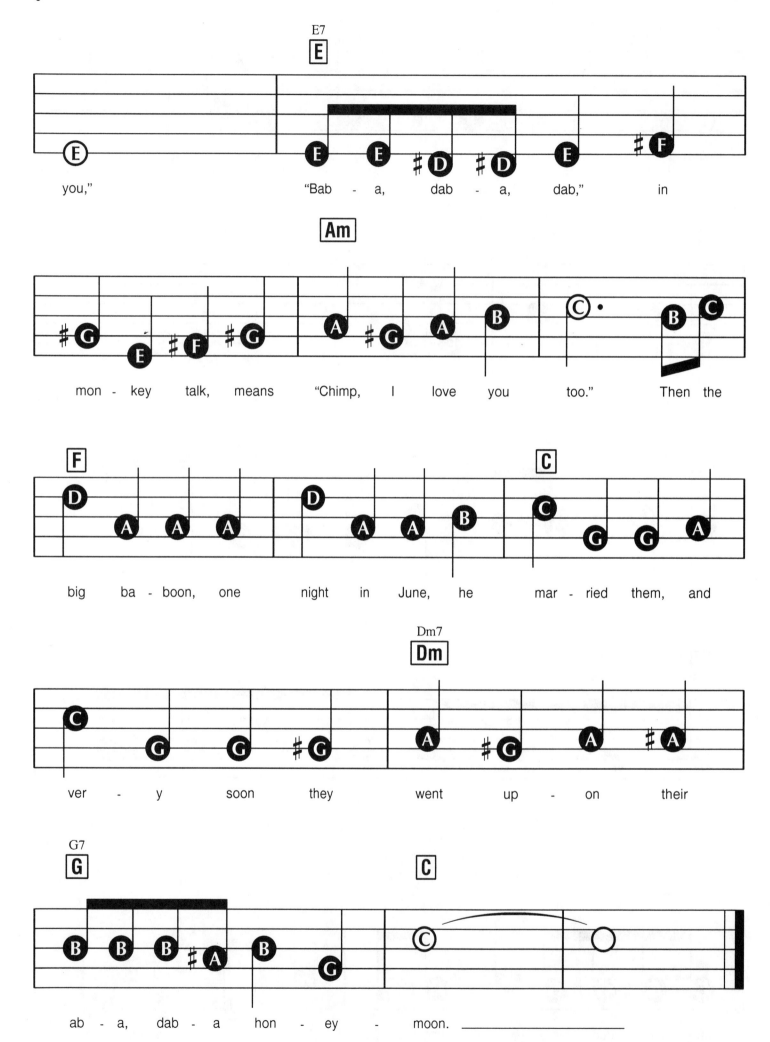

Chicago
(That Toddlin' Town)

Registration 7
Rhythm: Swing

Words and Music by
Fred Fisher

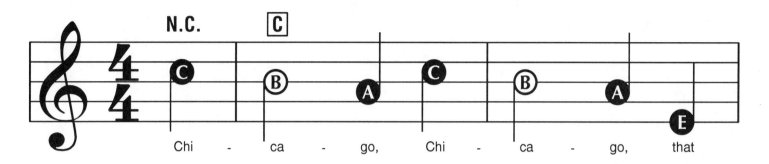

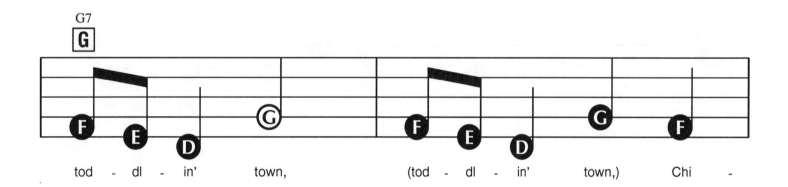

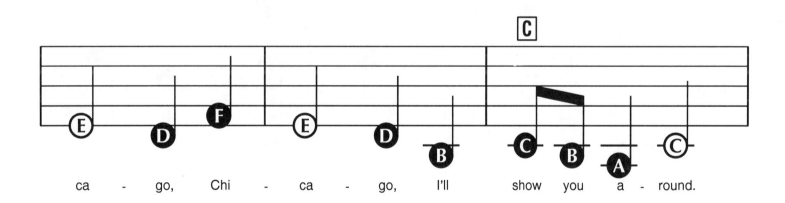

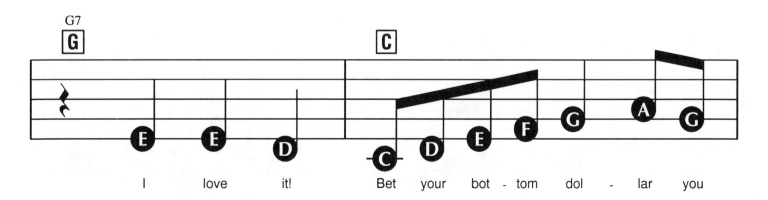

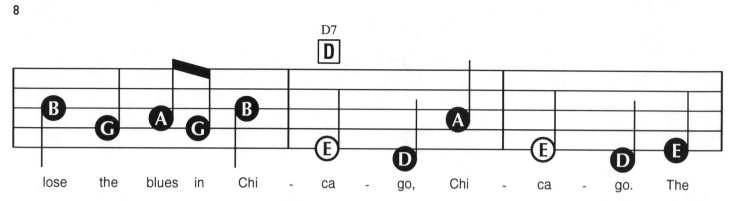

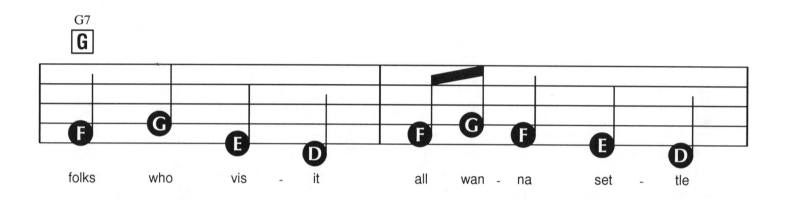

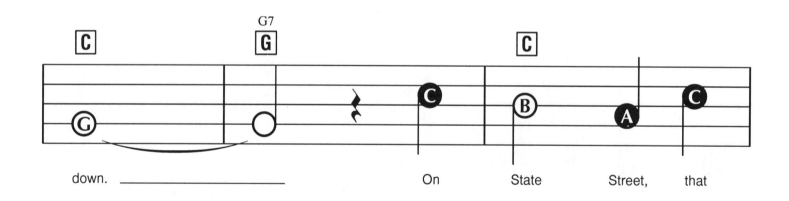

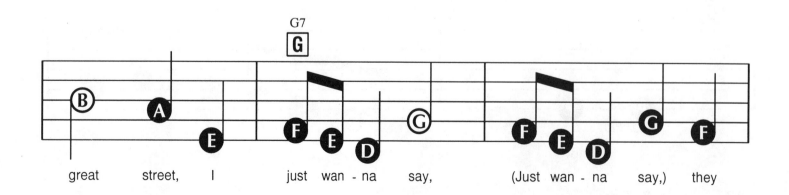

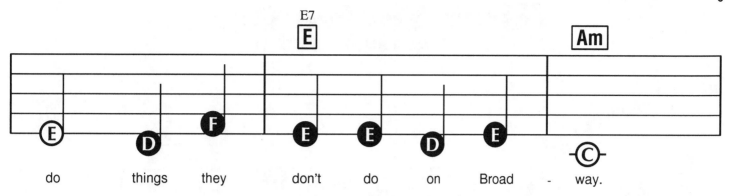

do things they don't do on Broad - way.

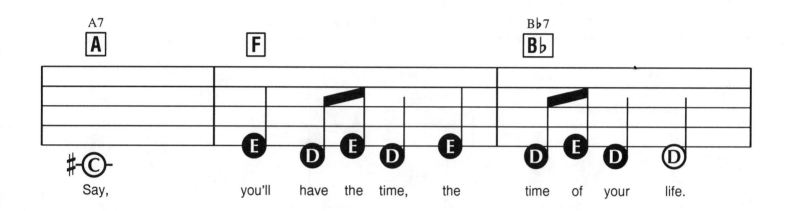

Say, you'll have the time, the time of your life.

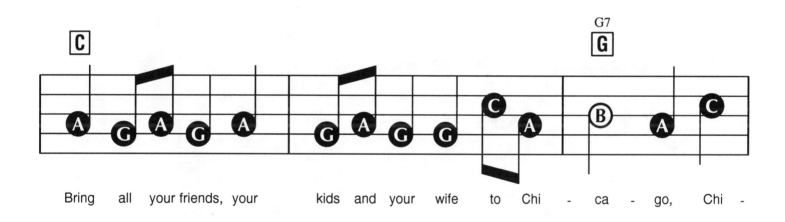

Bring all your friends, your kids and your wife to Chi - ca - go, Chi -

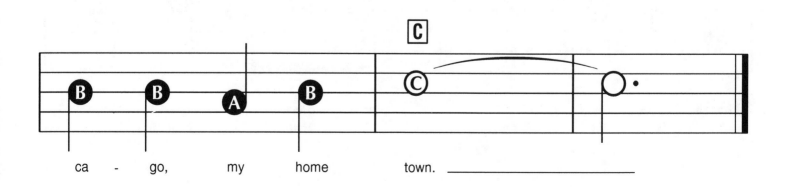

ca - go, my home town. _____

After You've Gone
from ONE MO' TIME

Words by Henry Creamer
Music by Turner Layton

Registration 8
Rhythm: Swing

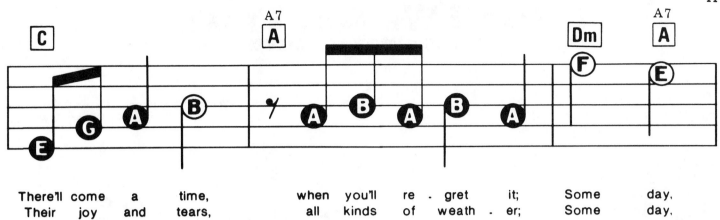

There'll come a time, when you'll re - gret it; Some day,
Their joy and tears, all kinds of weath - er; Some day,

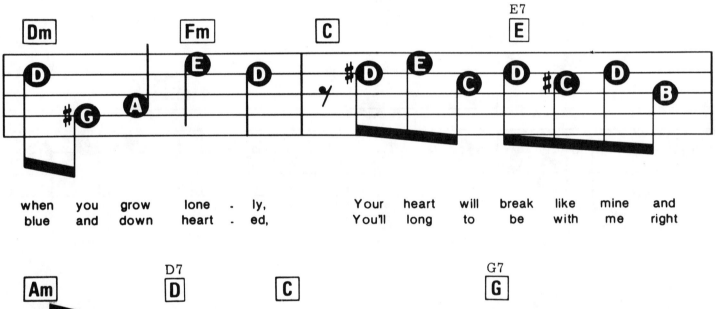

when you grow lone - ly, Your heart will break like mine and
blue and down heart - ed, You'll long to be with me right

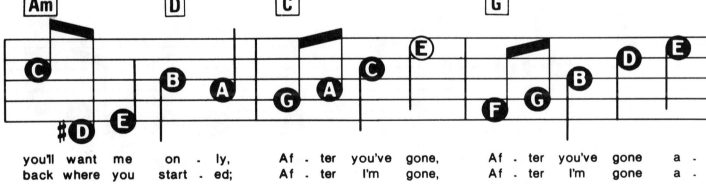

you'll want me on - ly, Af - ter you've gone, Af - ter you've gone a -
back where you start - ed; Af - ter I'm gone, Af - ter I'm gone a -

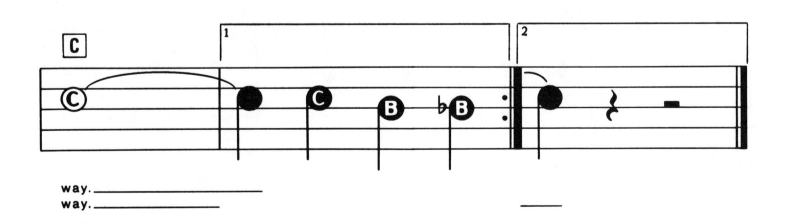

way._____
way._____

Ain't We Got Fun?

from BY THE LIGHT OF THE SILVERY MOON

Registration 5
Rhythm: Fox Trot or Swing

Words by Gus Kahn and Raymond B. Egan
Music by Richard A. Whiting

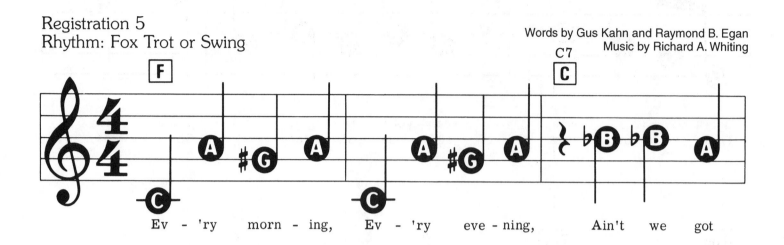

Ev - 'ry morn - ing, Ev - 'ry eve - ning, Ain't we got

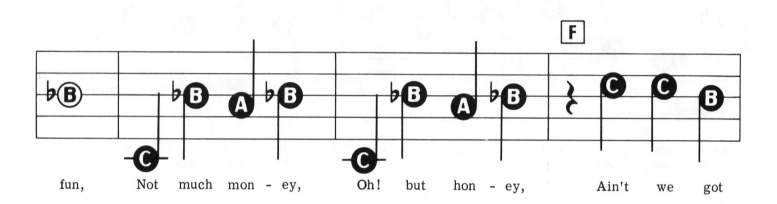

fun, Not much mon - ey, Oh! but hon - ey, Ain't we got

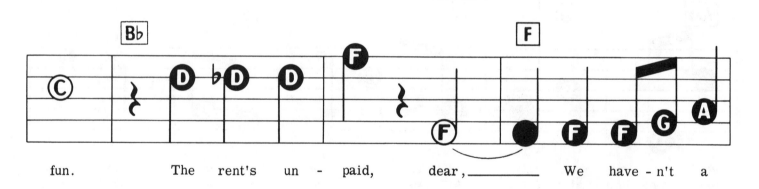

fun. The rent's un - paid, dear, _____ We have - n't a

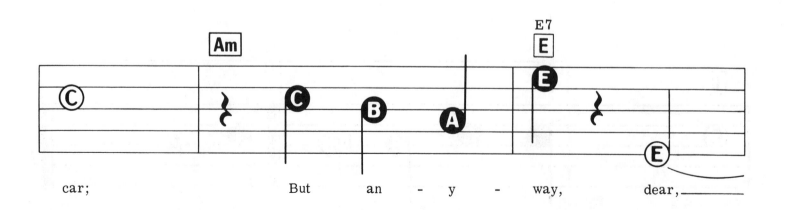

car; But an - y - way, dear, _____

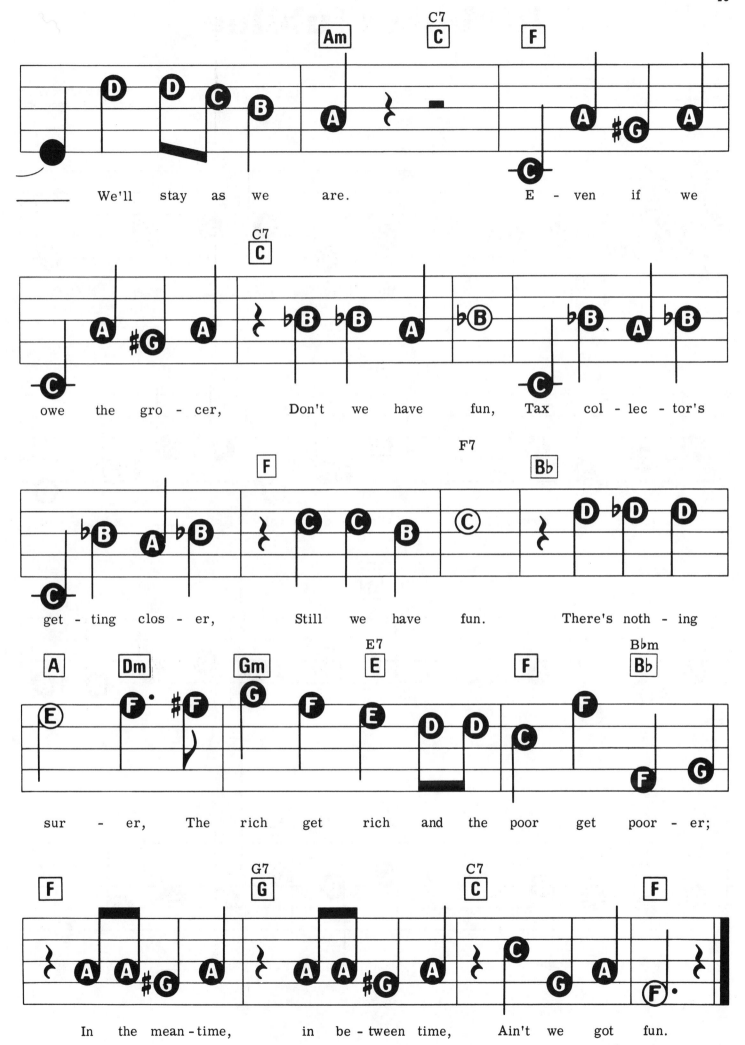

Alabama Jubilee

Registration 8
Rhythm: Swing

Words by Jack Yellen
Music by George Cobb

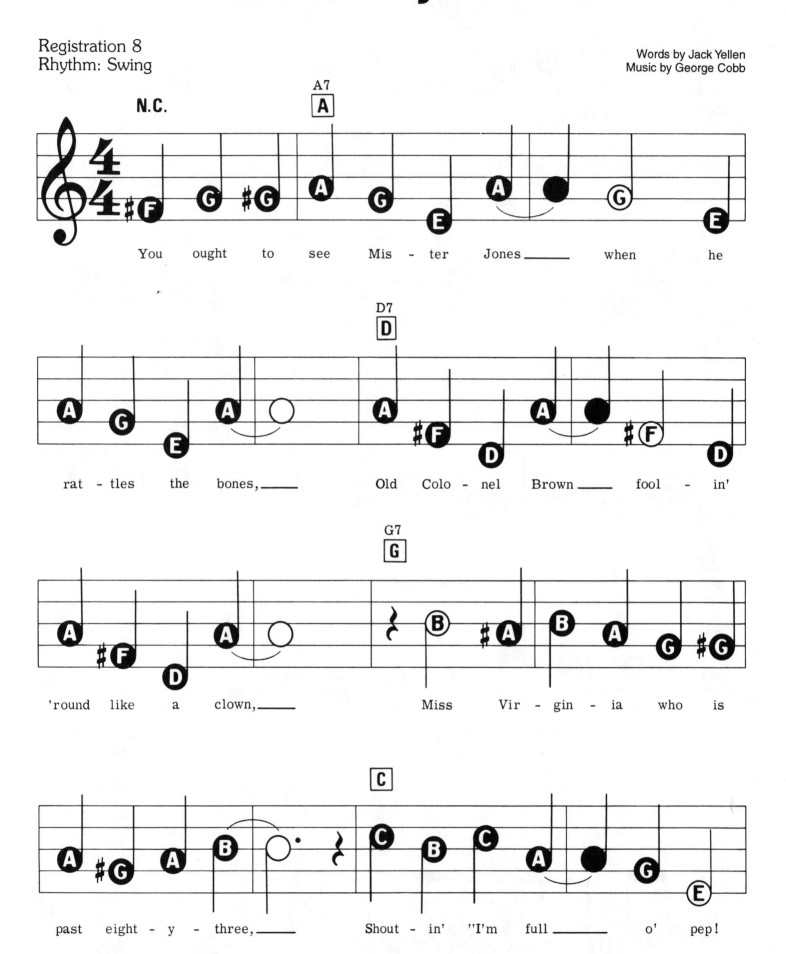

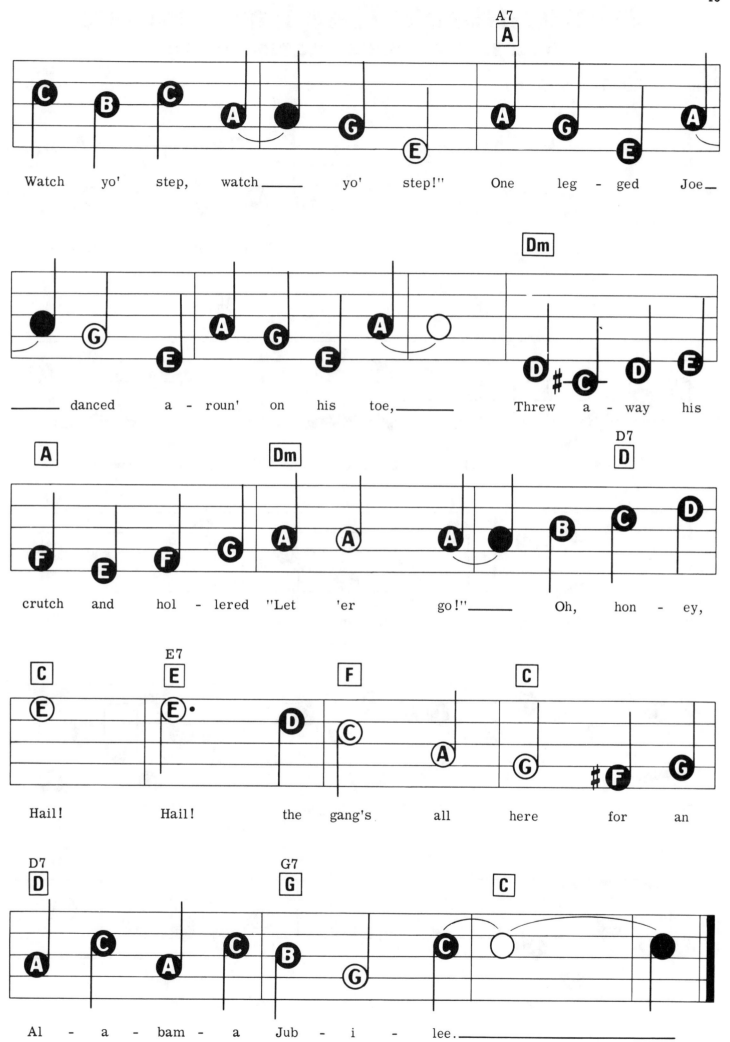

Alexander's Ragtime Band
from ALEXANDER'S RAGTIME BAND

Registration 5
Rhythm: Fox Trot or Swing

Words and Music by
Irving Berlin

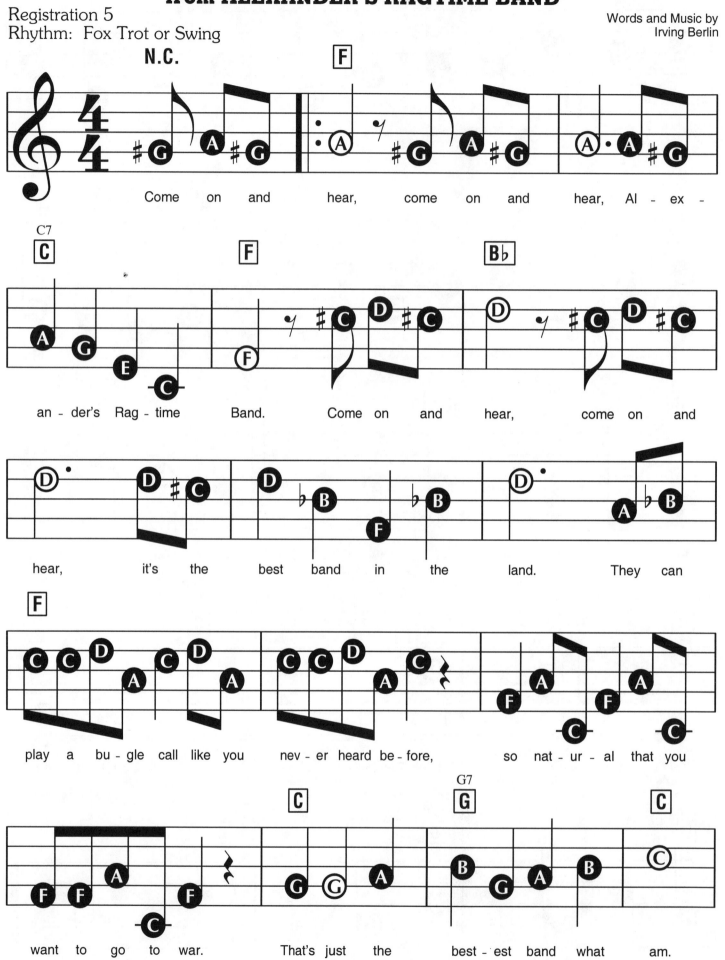

17

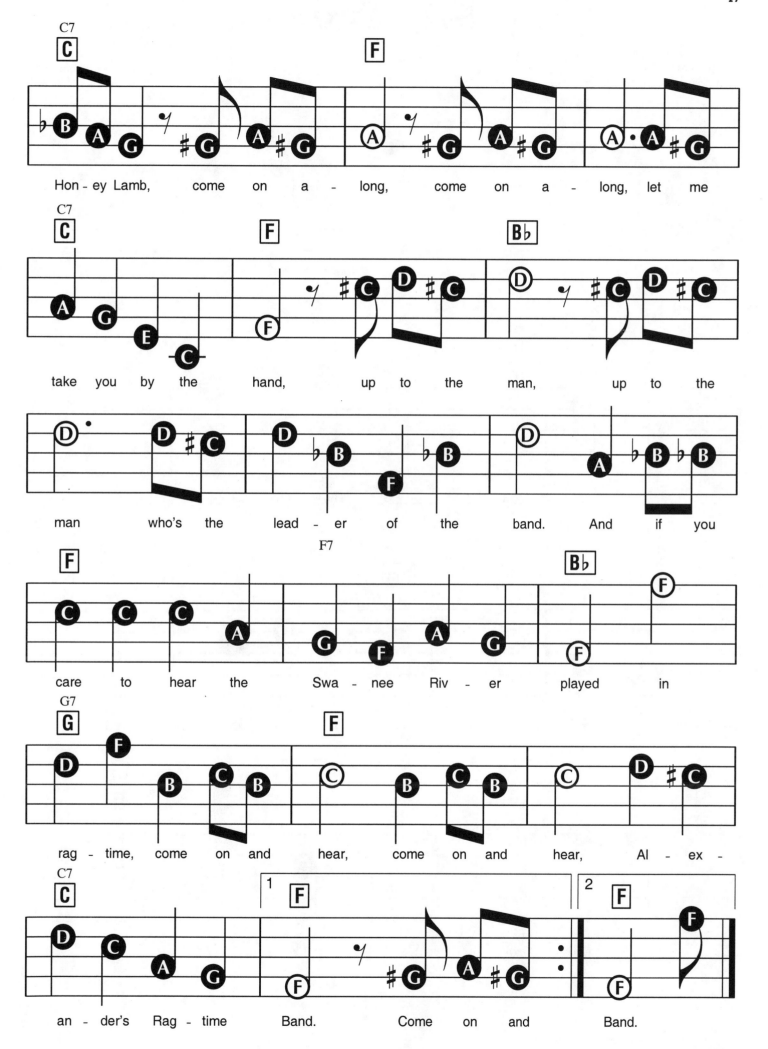

Any Time

Registration 3
Rhythm: Shuffle or Swing

Words and Music by
Herbert Happy Lawson

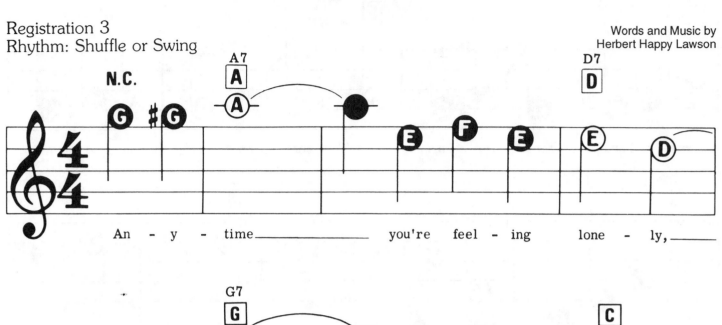

An - y - time _____ you're feel - ing lone - ly, _____

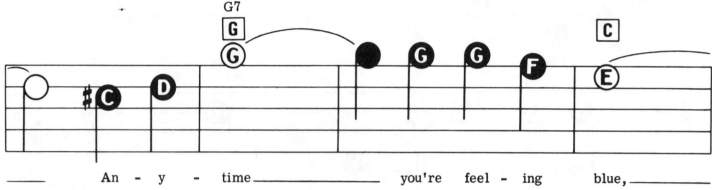

_____ An - y - time _____ you're feel - ing blue, _____

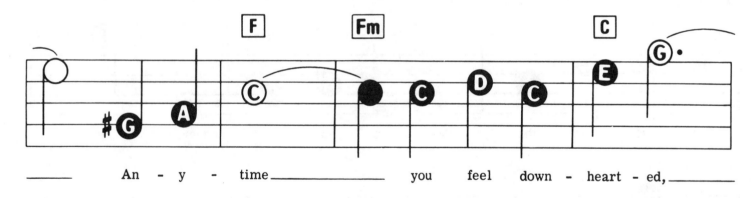

_____ An - y - time _____ you feel down - heart - ed, _____

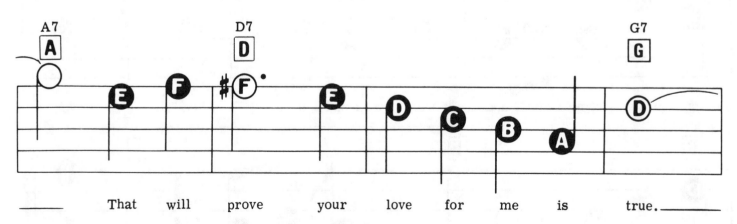

_____ That will prove your love for me is true. _____

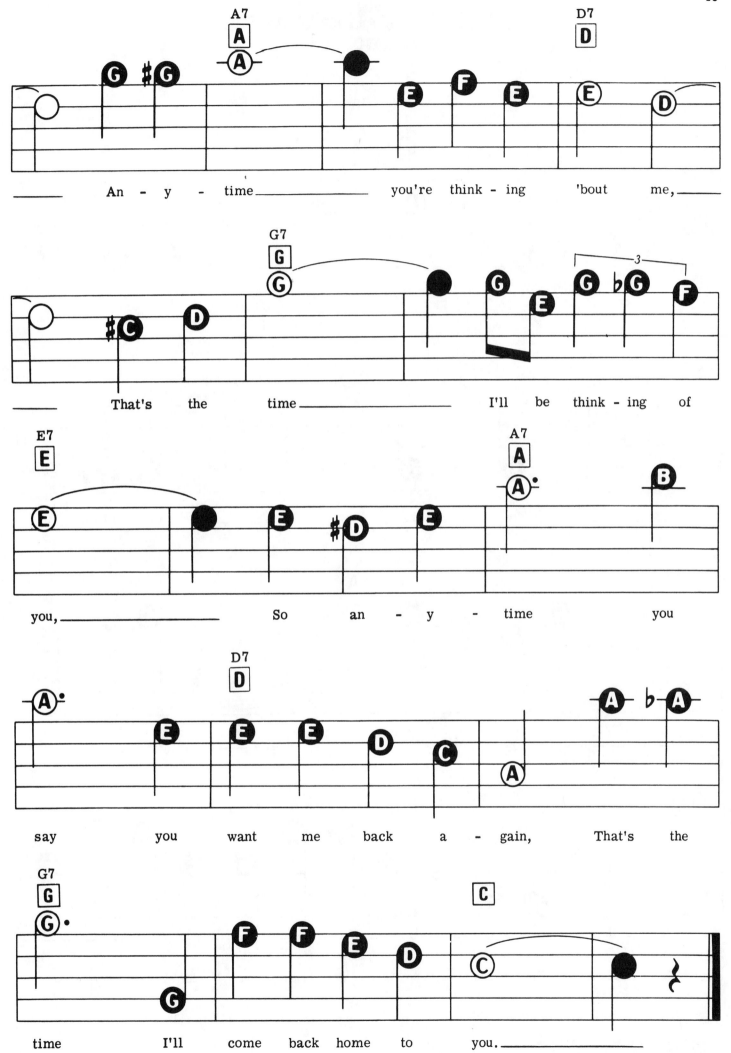

April Showers
from BOMBO

Registration 9
Rhythm: Swing

Words by B.G. DeSylva
Music by Louis Silvers

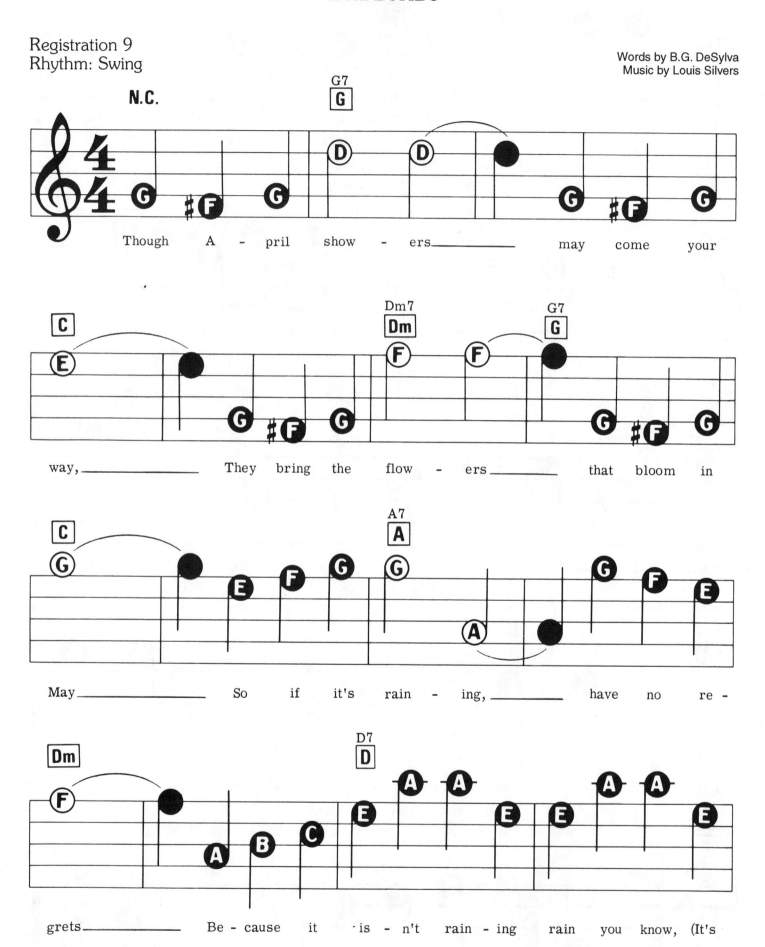

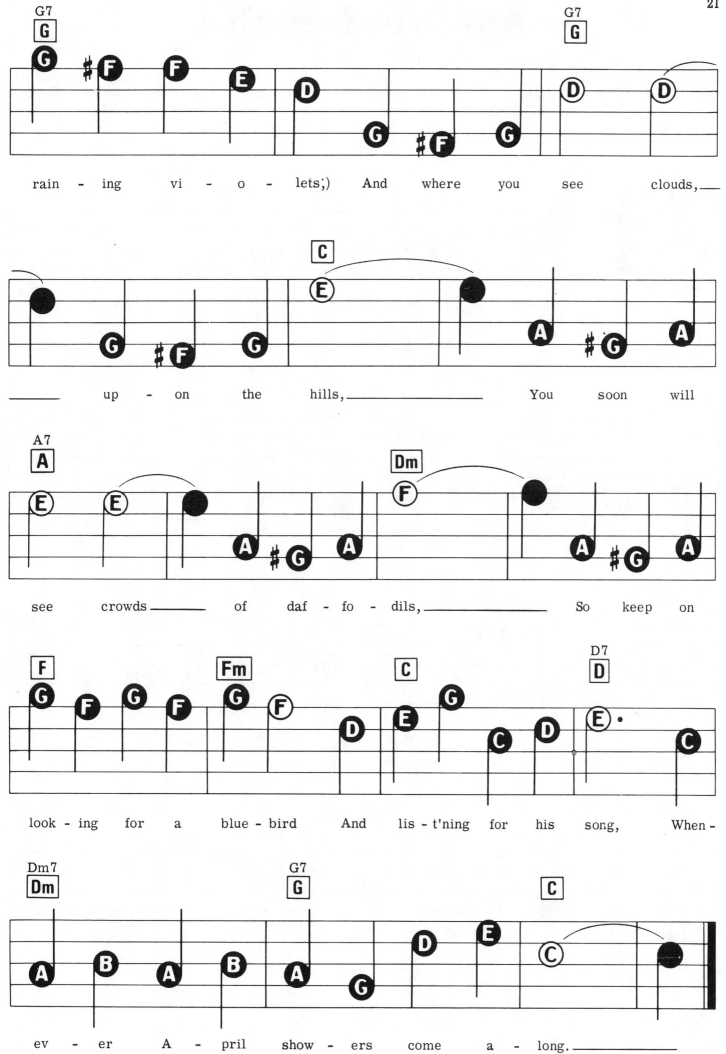

Auf Wiedersehn

Registration 6
Rhythm: Waltz or Jazz Waltz

Words by Herbert Reynolds
Music by Sigmund Romberg

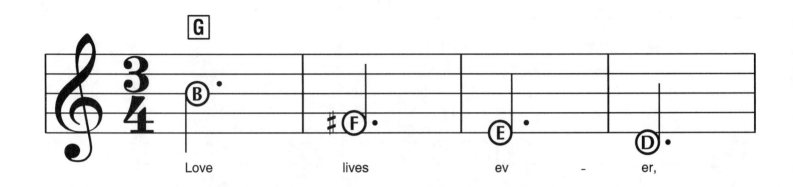

Love   lives   ev – er,

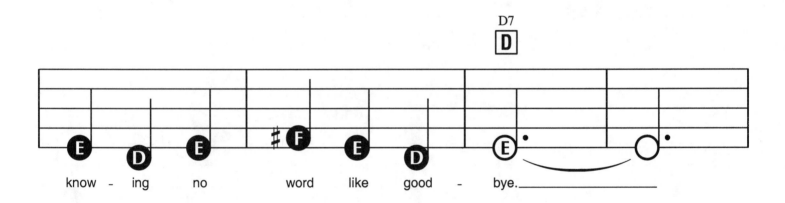

know – ing   no   word   like   good – bye._____

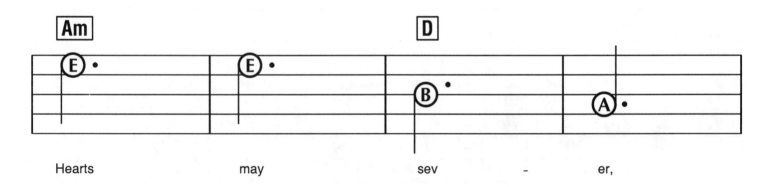

Hearts   may   sev – er,

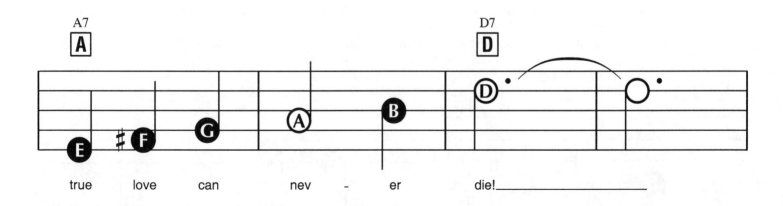

true   love   can   nev – er   die!_____

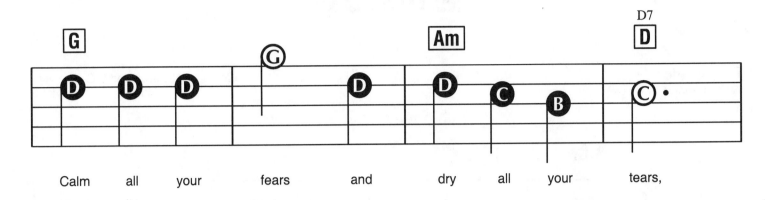

Calm all your fears and dry all your tears,

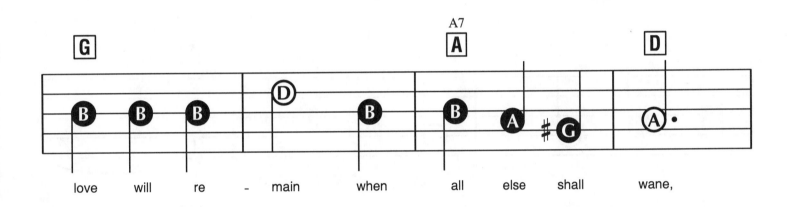

love will re - main when all else shall wane,

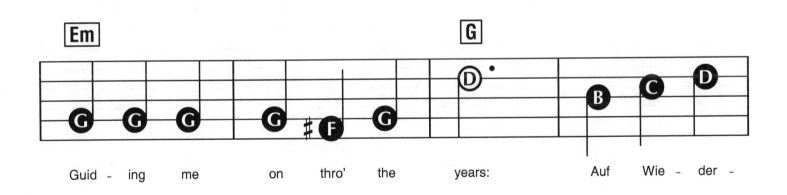

Guid - ing me on thro' the years: Auf Wie - der -

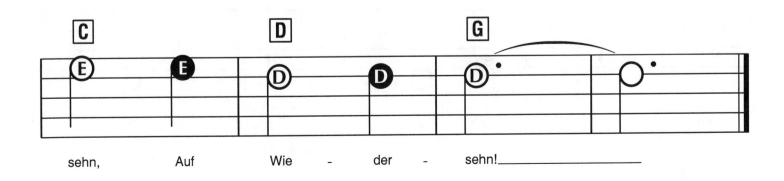

sehn, Auf Wie - der - sehn!_____

Avalon

Registration 9
Rhythm: Swing

Words by Al Jolson and B.G. DeSylva
Music by Vincent Rose

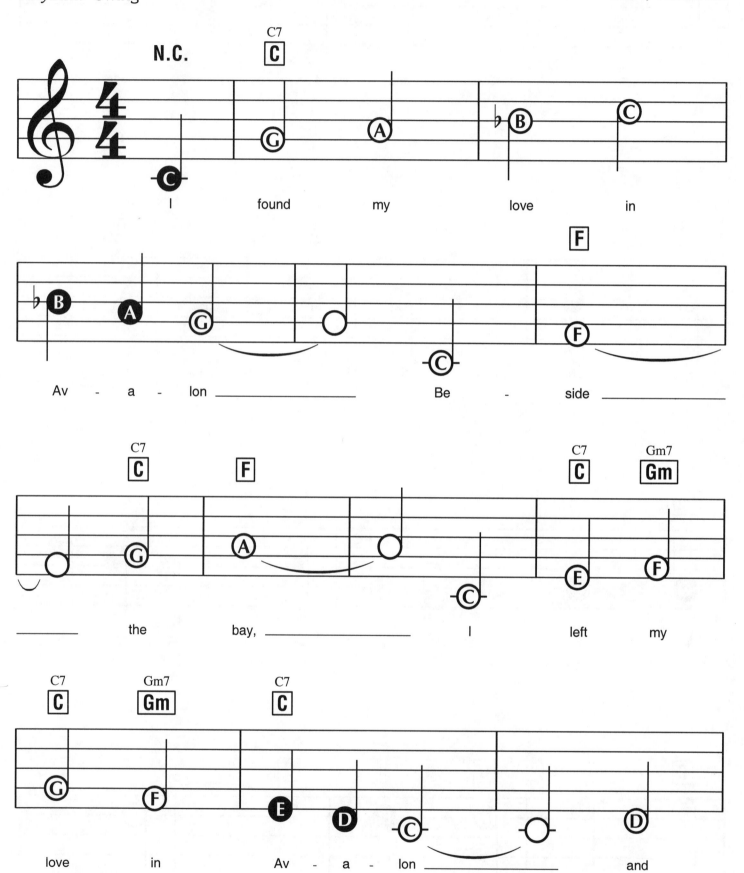

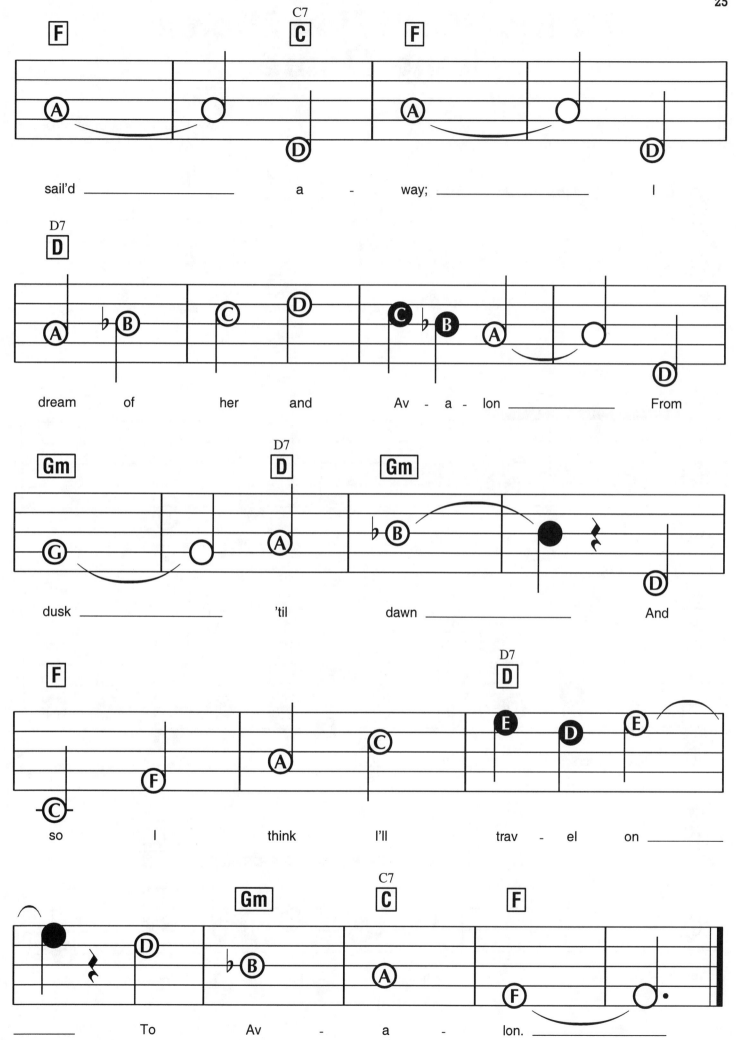

Baby, Won't You Please Come Home

Registration 7
Rhythm: Fox Trot or Swing

Words and Music by Charles Warfield
and Clarence Williams

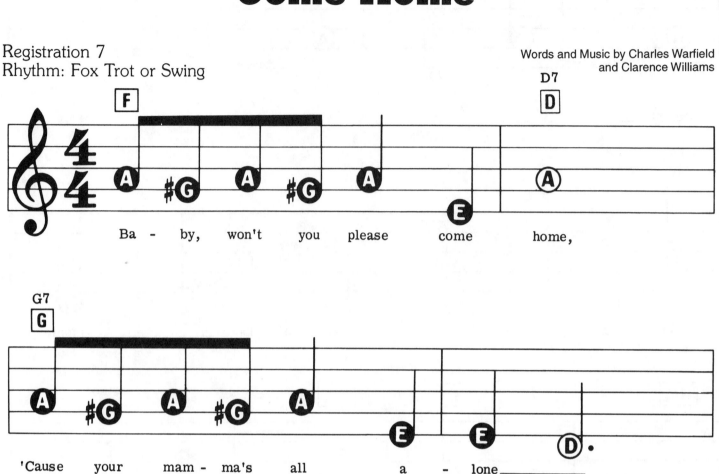

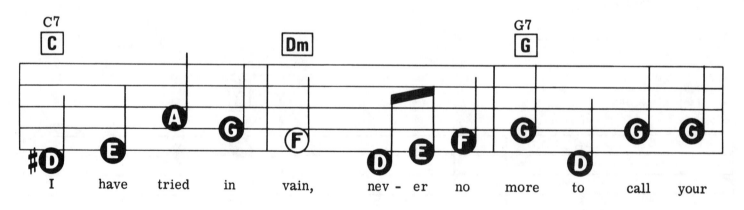

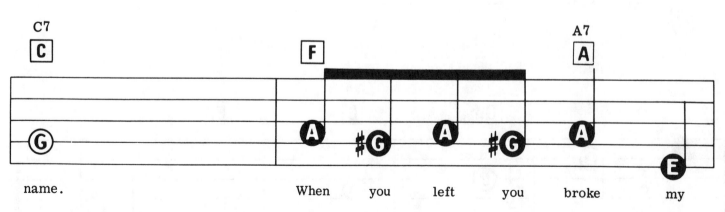

By the Light of the Silvery Moon

Registration 2
Rhythm: Swing

Lyrics by Ed Madden
Music by Gus Edwards

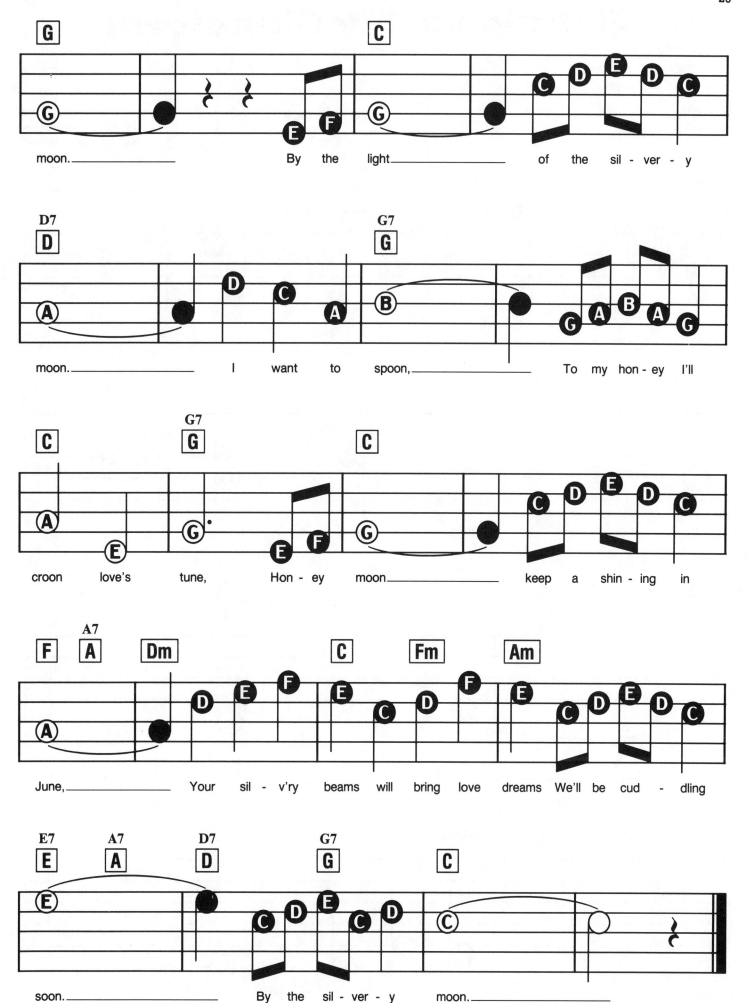

Chinatown, My Chinatown

Registration 4
Rhythm: Swing

Words by William Jerome
Music by Jean Schwartz

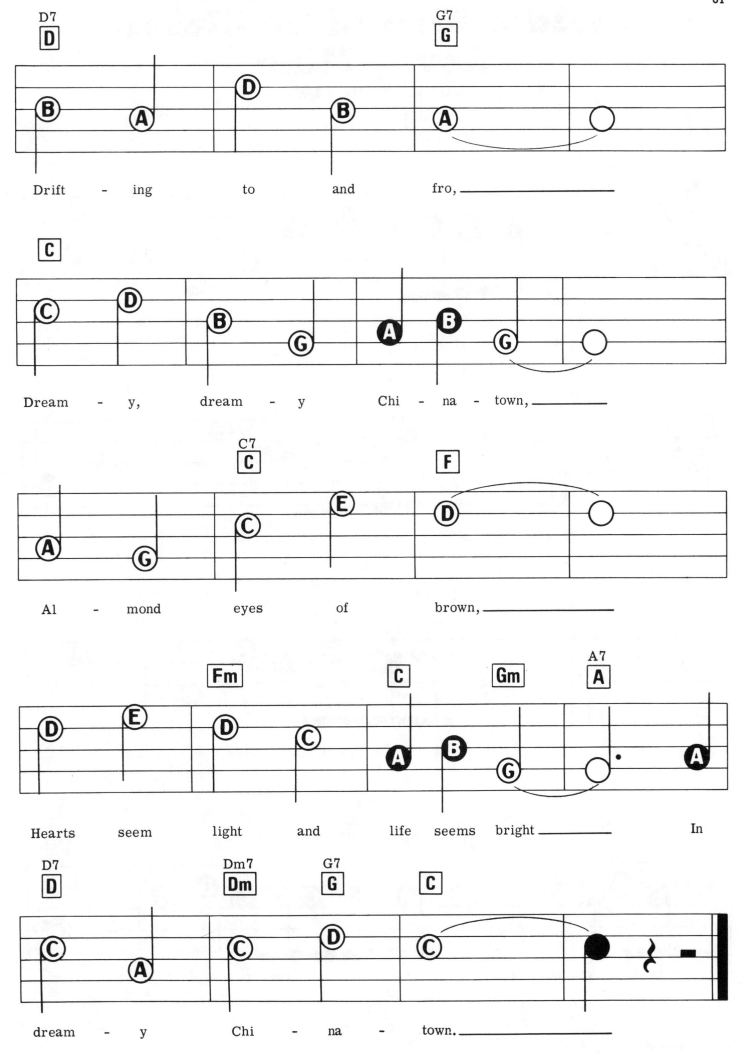

Cuddle Up a Little Closer, Lovey Mine

from THE THREE TWINS

Registration 3
Rhythm: Swing

Words by Otto Harbach
Music by Karl Hoschna

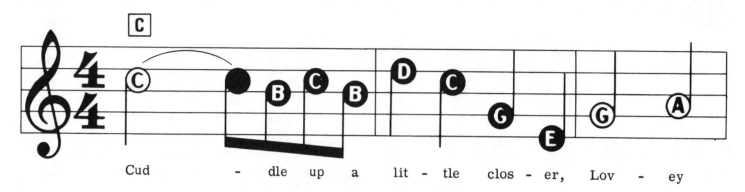

Cud - dle up a lit - tle clos - er, Lov - ey

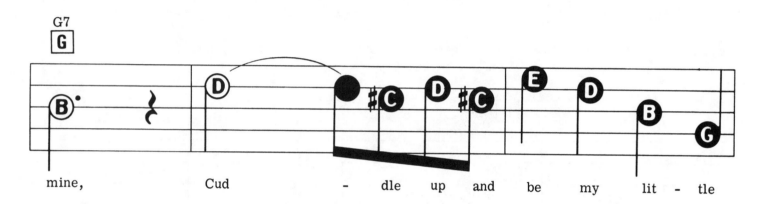

mine, Cud - dle up and be my lit - tle

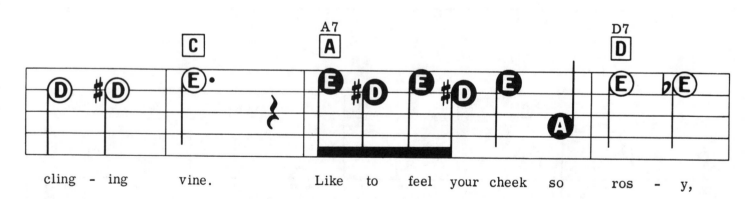

cling - ing vine. Like to feel your cheek so ros - y,

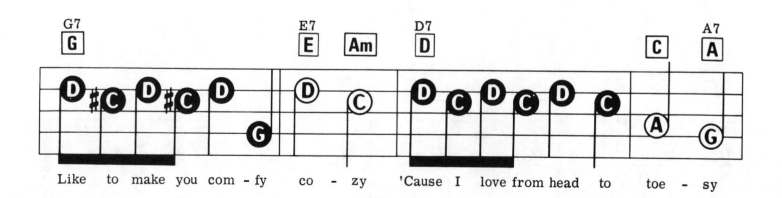

Like to make you com - fy co - zy 'Cause I love from head to toe - sy

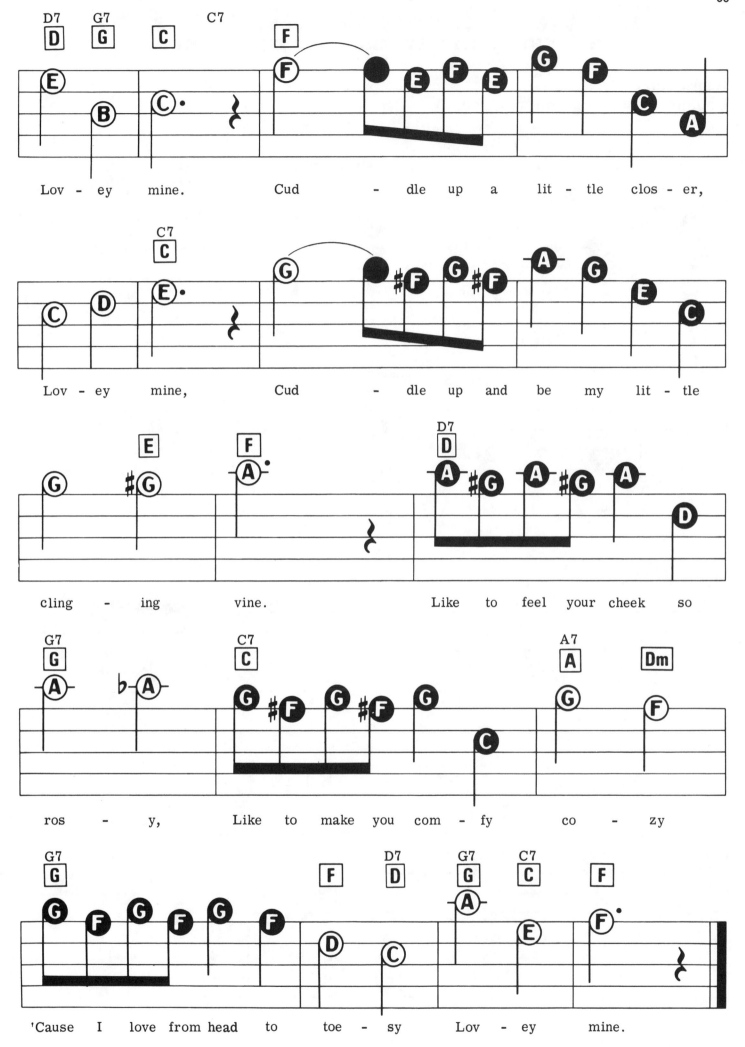

The Darktown Strutters' Ball
from THE STORY OF VERNON AND IRENE CASTLE

Registration 8
Rhythm: Polka, Fox Trot, or Dixie

Words and Music by
Shelton Brooks

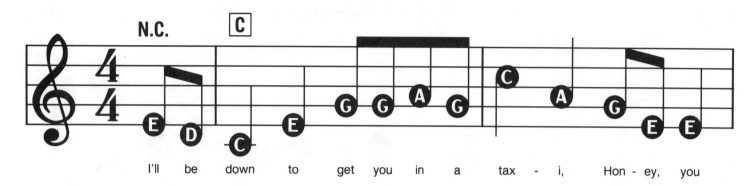

I'll be down to get you in a tax - i, Hon - ey, you

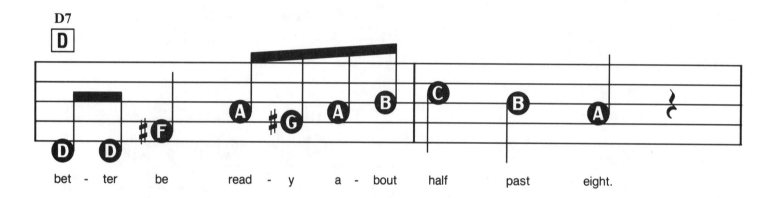

bet - ter be read - y a - bout half past eight.

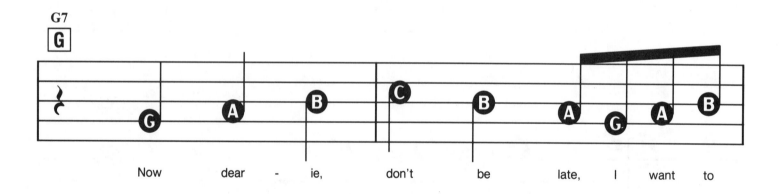

Now dear - ie, don't be late, I want to

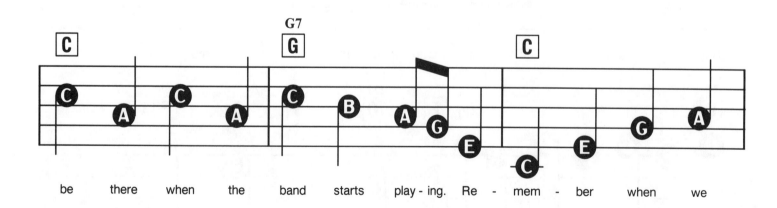

be there when the band starts play - ing. Re - mem - ber when we

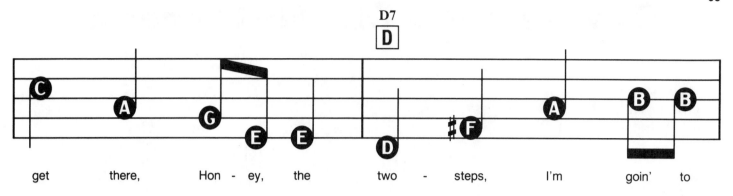

get there, Hon - ey, the two - steps, I'm goin' to

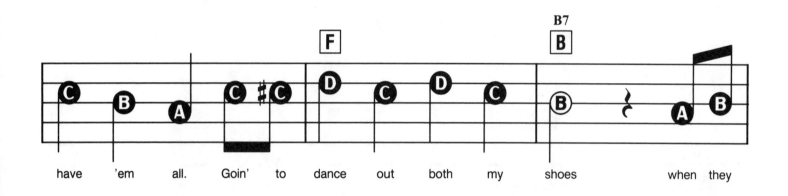

have 'em all. Goin' to dance out both my shoes when they

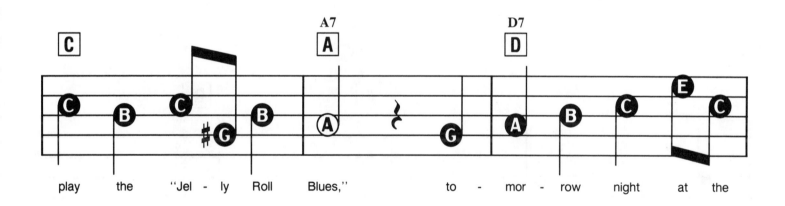

play the "Jel - ly Roll Blues," to - mor - row night at the

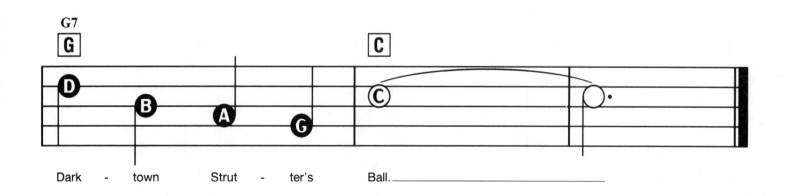

Dark - town Strut - ter's Ball._____

Down by the Old Mill Stream

Registration 3
Rhythm: Waltz

Words and Music by
Tell Taylor

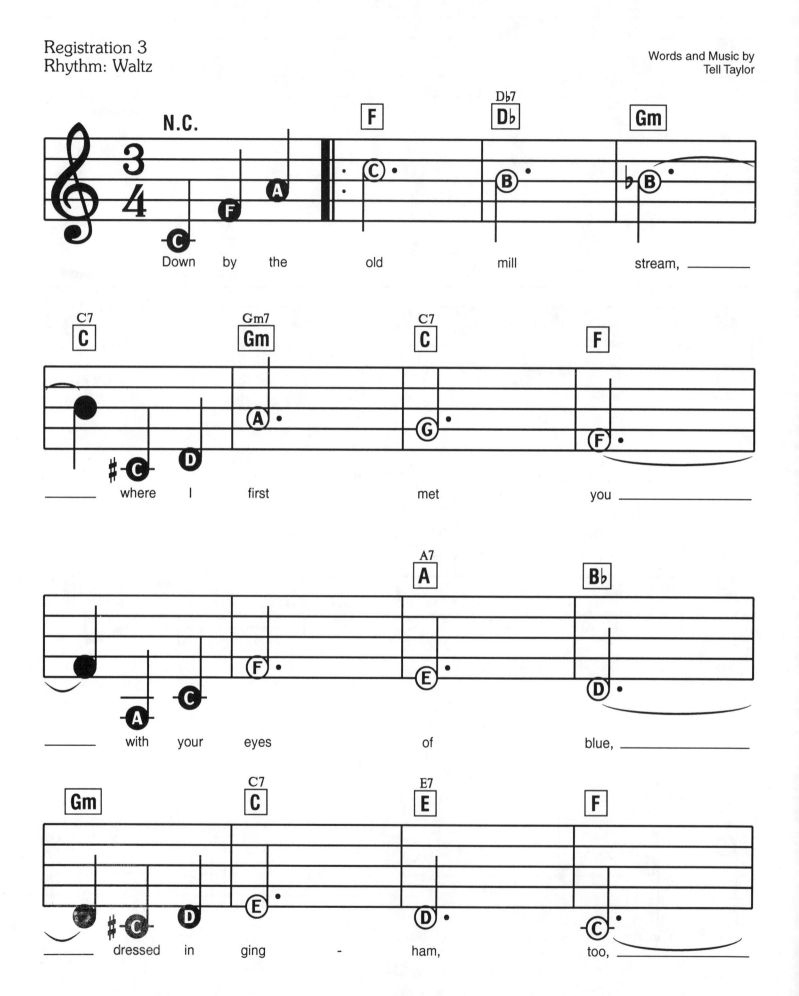

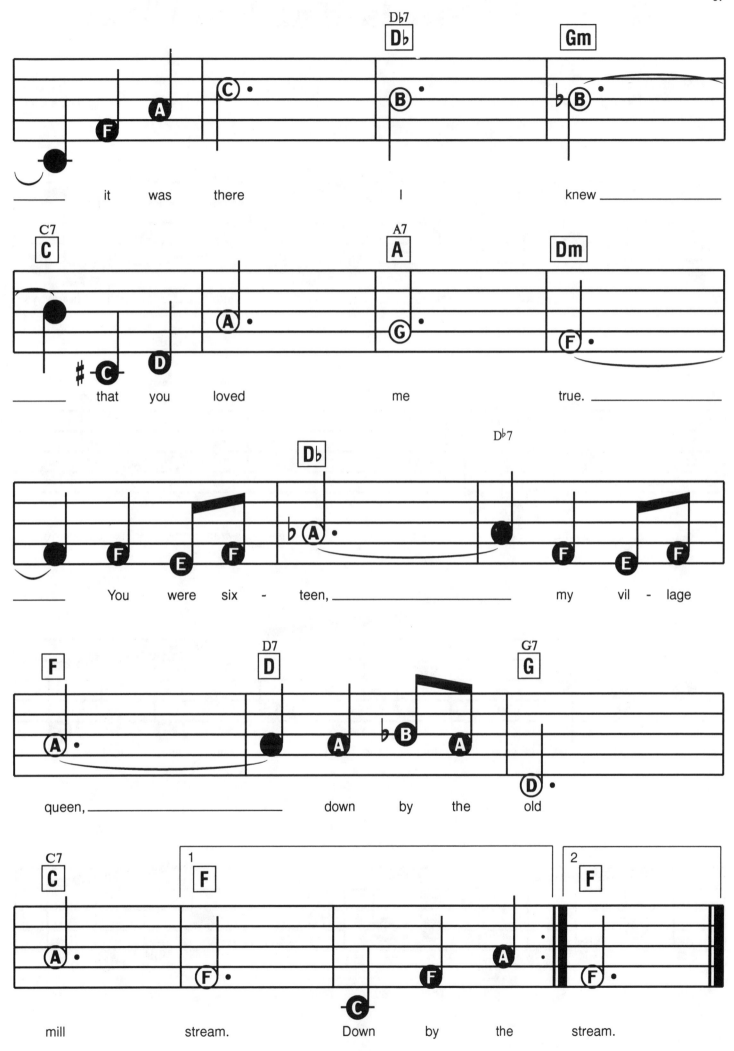

A Good Man Is Hard to Find

Registration 5
Rhythm: 2-Beat, Swing, or Shuffle

Words and Music by
Eddie Green

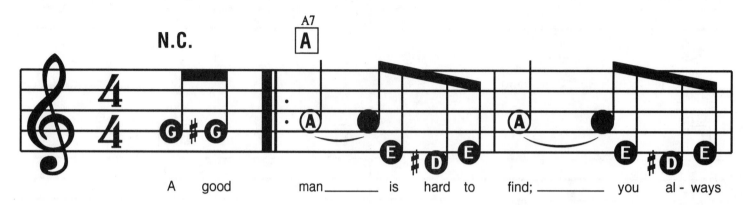

A good man is hard to find; you al-ways

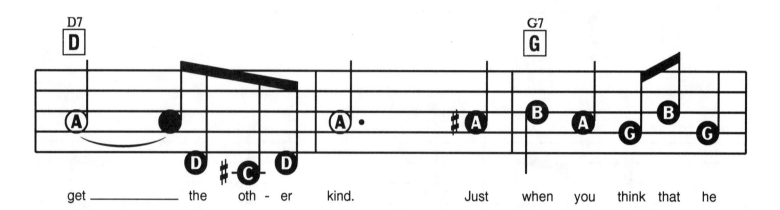

get the oth-er kind. Just when you think that he

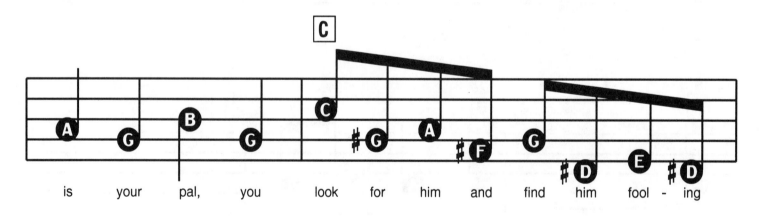

is your pal, you look for him and find him fool-ing

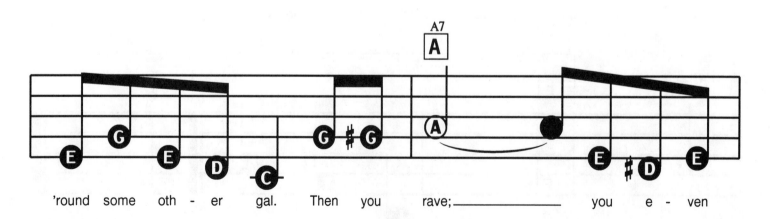

'round some oth-er gal. Then you rave; you e-ven

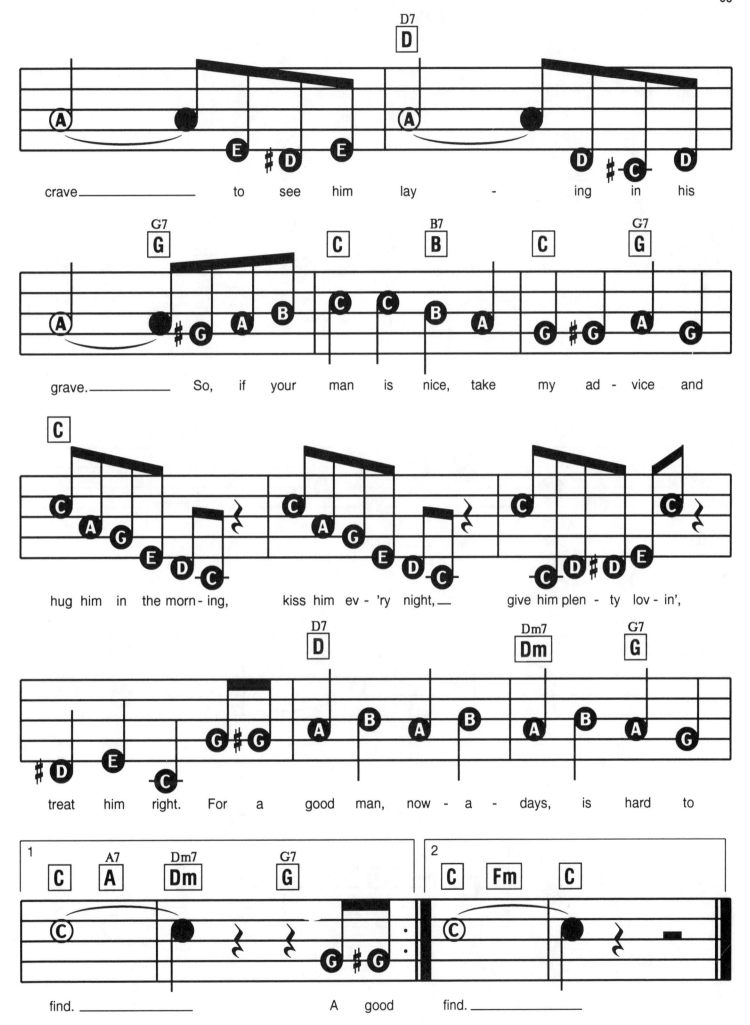

Hindustan

Registration 4
Rhythm: Fox Trot or Show Beat

Words and Music by Oliver Wallace
and Harold Weeks

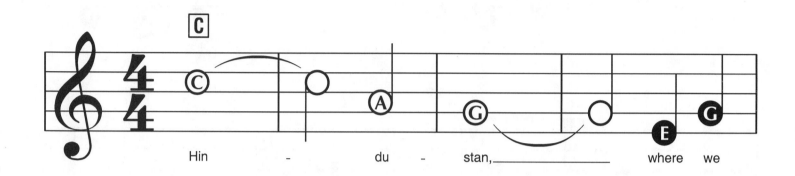

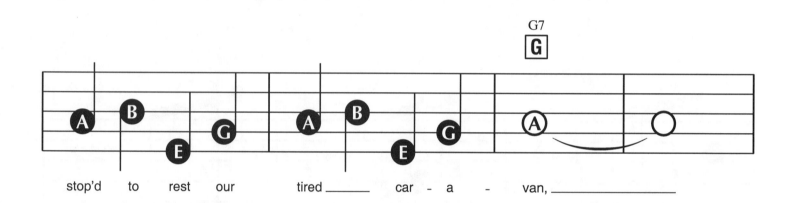

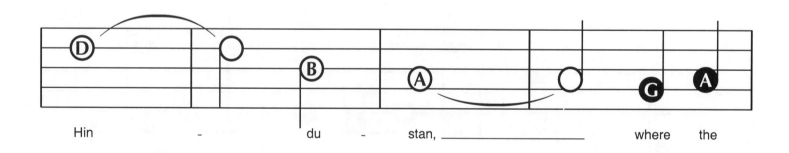

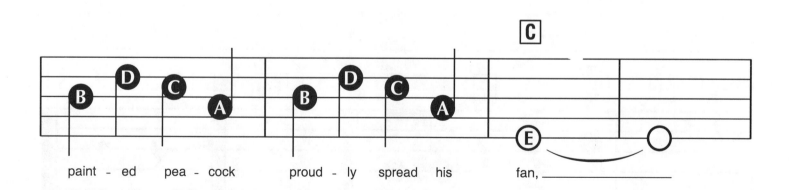

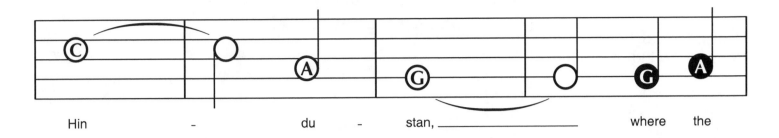

Hin - du - stan, _____ where the

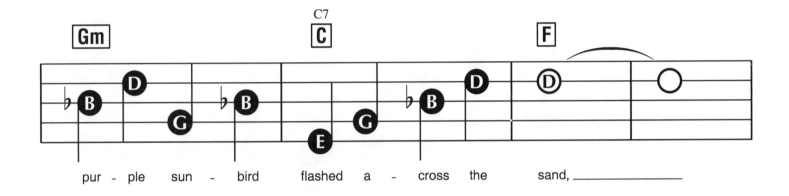

pur - ple sun - bird flashed a - cross the sand, _____

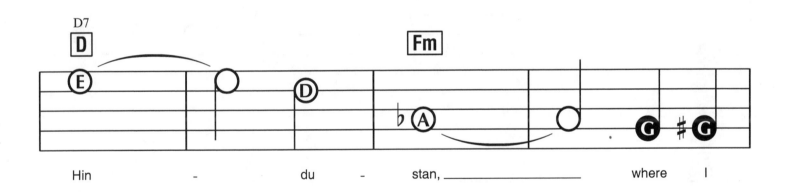

Hin - du - stan, _____ where I

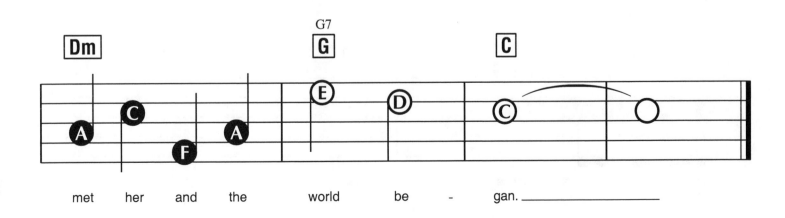

met her and the world be - gan. _____

I Ain't Got Nobody
(And Nobody Cares for Me)

Registration 8
Rhythm: Swing or Shuffle

Words by Roger Graham
Music by Spencer Williams and Dave Peyton

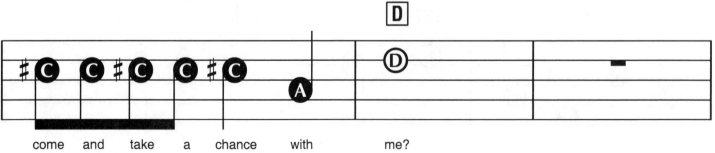

43

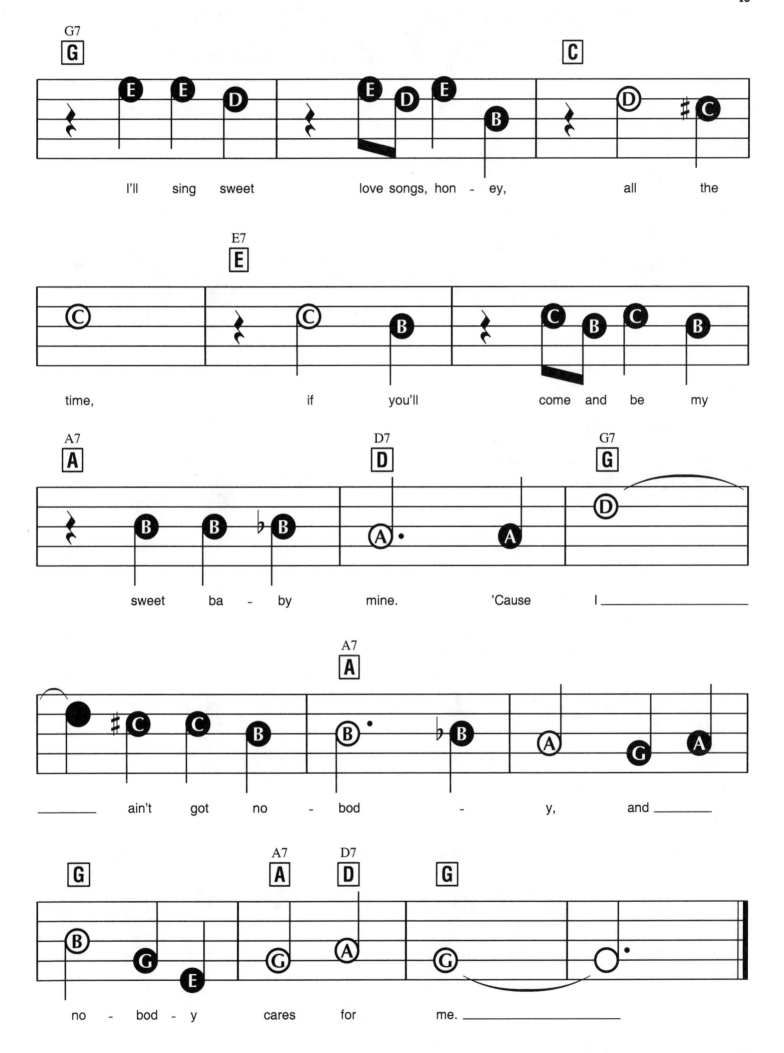

I Wish I Could Shimmy Like My Sister Kate

Registration 8
Rhythm: Shuffle or Swing

Words and Music by
Armand J. Piron

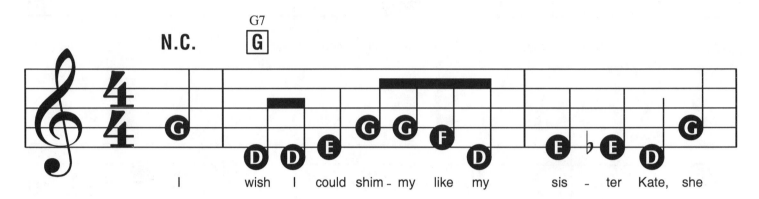

I wish I could shim-my like my sis - ter Kate, she

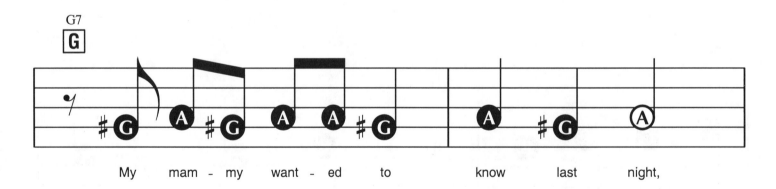

shiv - ers like the jel - ly on a plate.

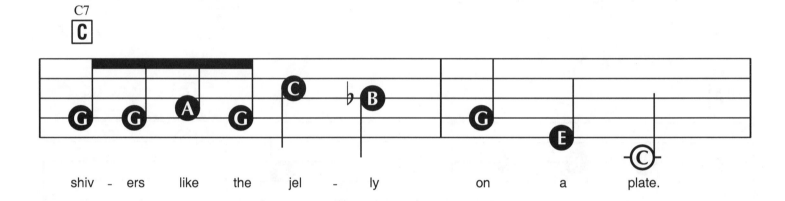

My mam-my want-ed to know last night,

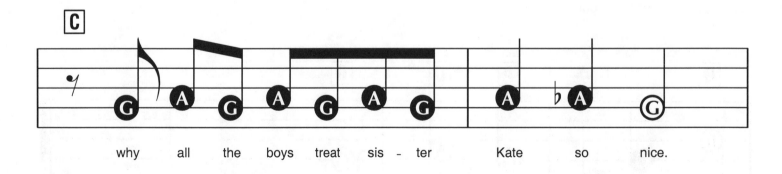

why all the boys treat sis - ter Kate so nice.

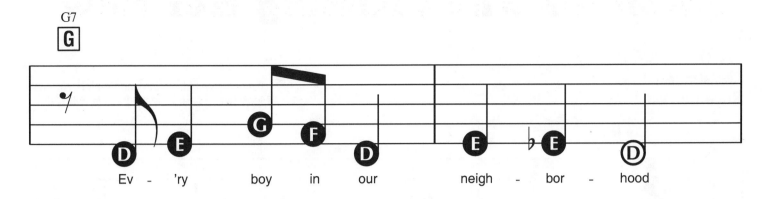

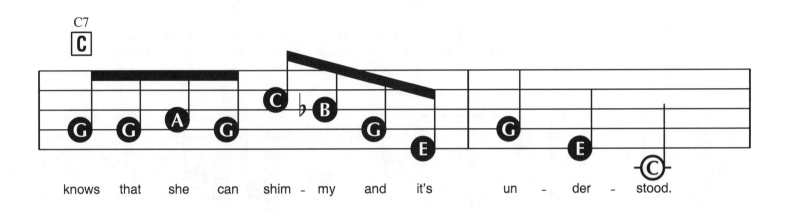

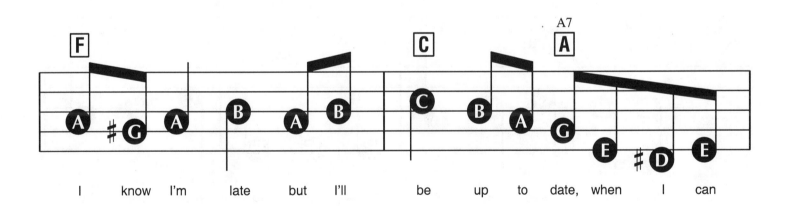

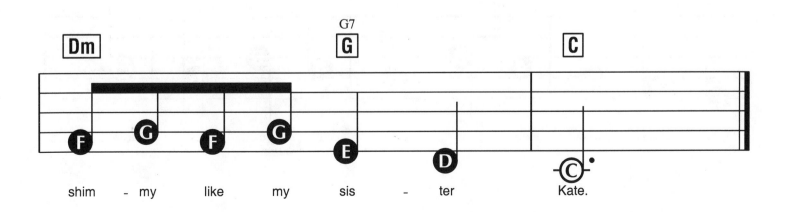

I Wonder Who's Kissing Her Now

Registration 1
Rhythm: Waltz

Lyrics by Will M. Hough and Frank R. Adams
Music by Joseph E. Howard and Harold Orlob

N.C.   **G**

B   C   D   E   #C   D   E   #C   D   E   #F

You have loved lots of girls in the sweet long a-
kissed 'neath the moon while the world seemed in

G   A   B   D   B   A   G   #F   G   B

go And each one has meant Heav - en to you,_____
tune, Then you've left her to hunt a new game_____

1   **Am**

B   B   C   B   A   E   E   E   C   B   A

_____ You have vowed your af - fec - tion to each one in
_____ Does it

A7   **A**   D7   **D**

E   #F   G   A   B   G   A   B   G   A

turn And have sworn to them all you'd be true;_____

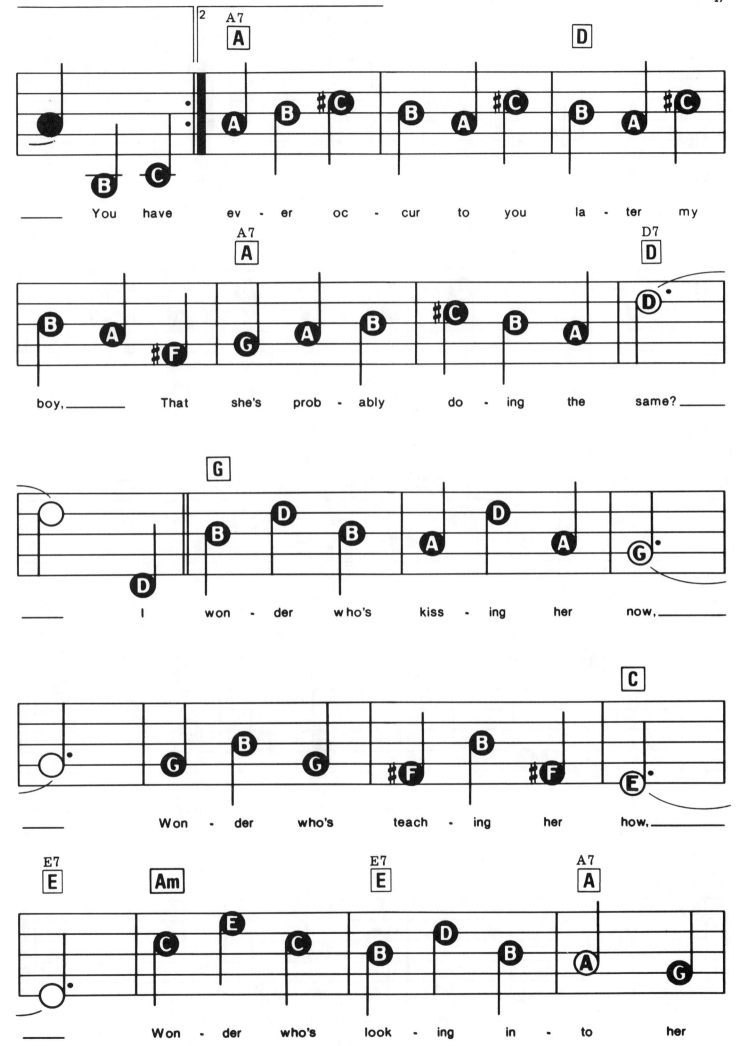

48

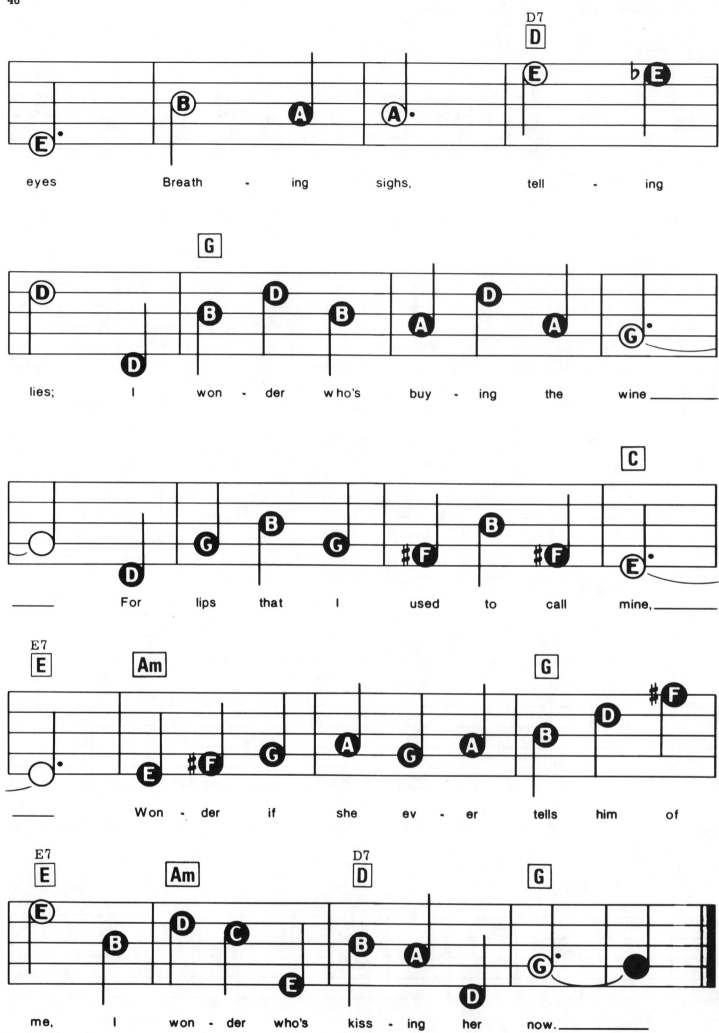

Johnson Rag

Registration 5
Rhythm: Swing

Words by Jack Lawrence
Music by Guy Hall and Henry Kleinkauf

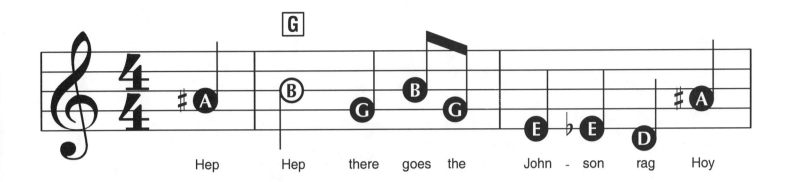

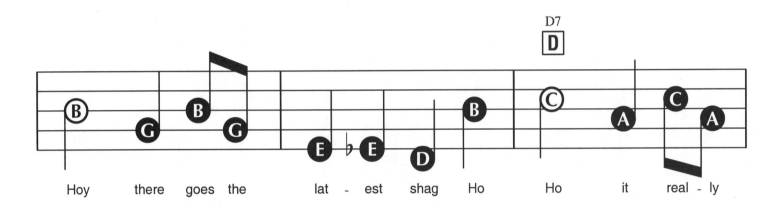

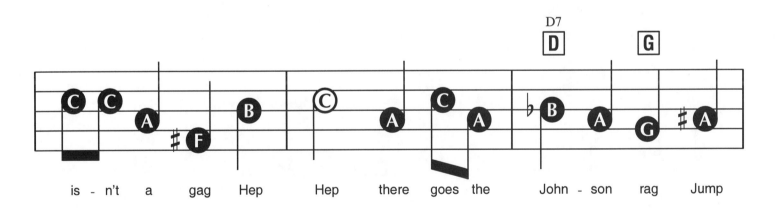

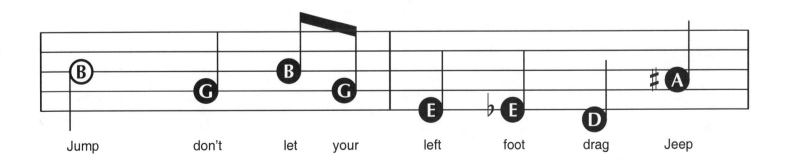

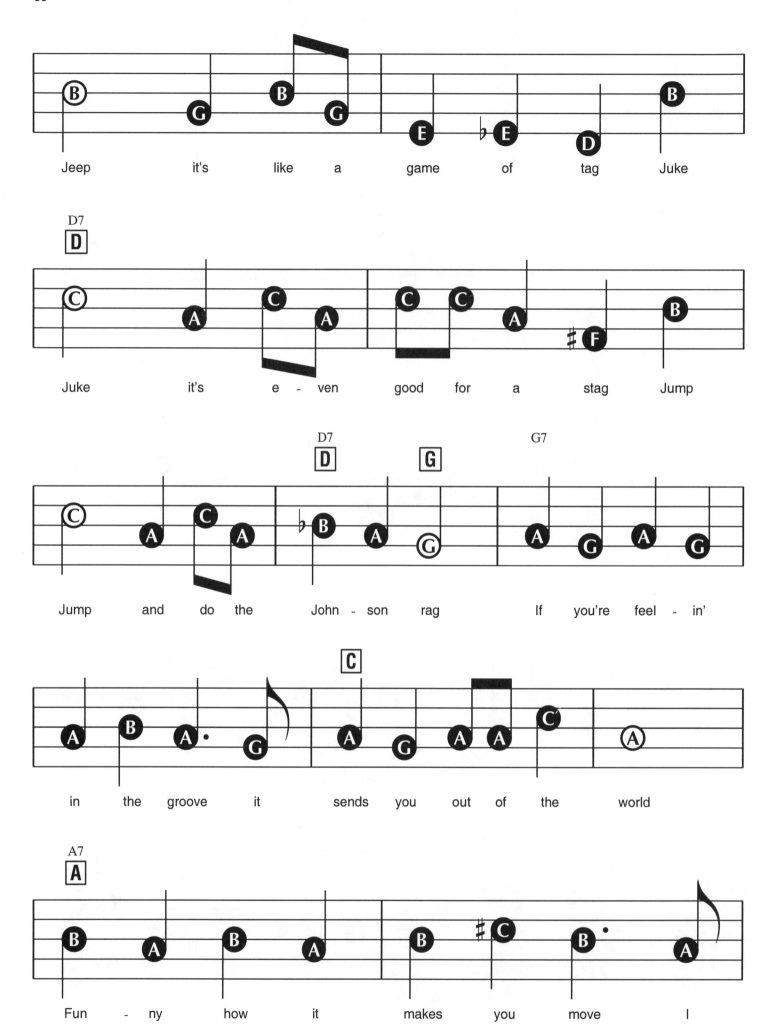

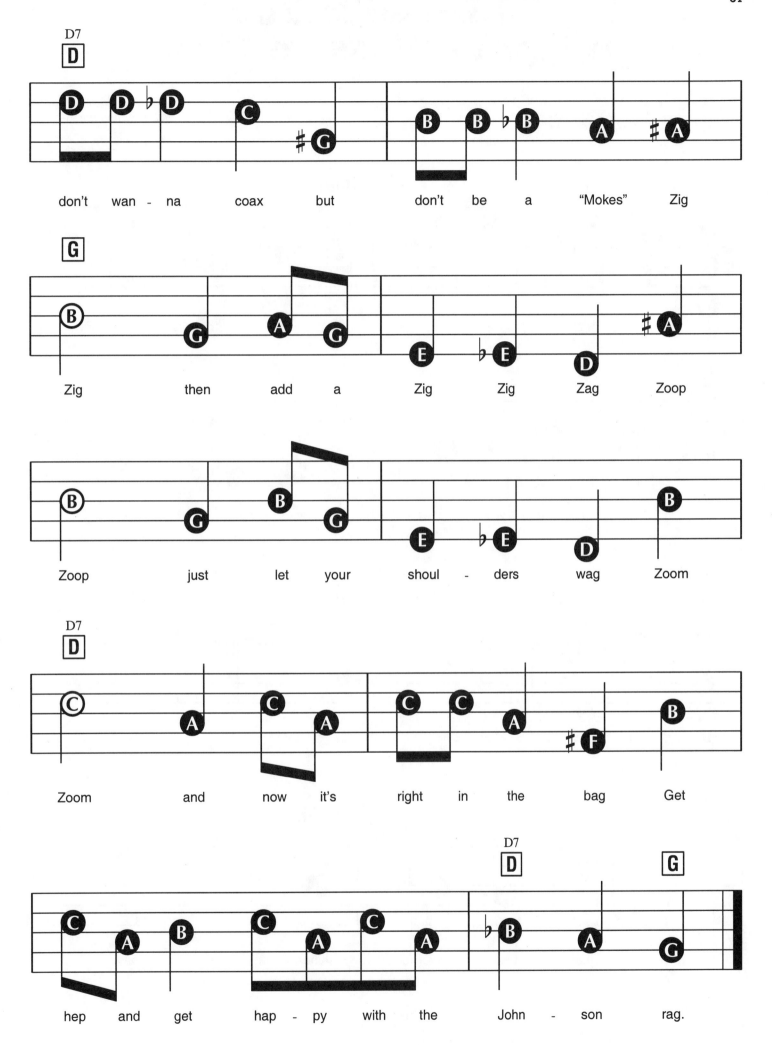

I'll Be with You in Apple Blossom Time

Registration 4
Rhythm: Waltz or Jazz Waltz

Words by Neville Fleeson
Music by Albert von Tilzer

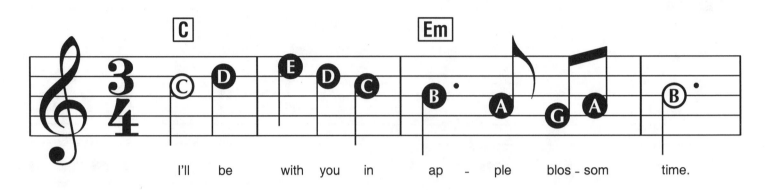

I'll be with you in ap - ple blos - som time.

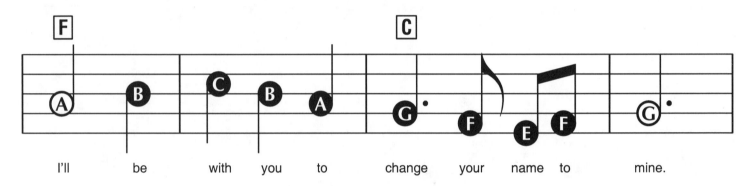

I'll be with you to change your name to mine.

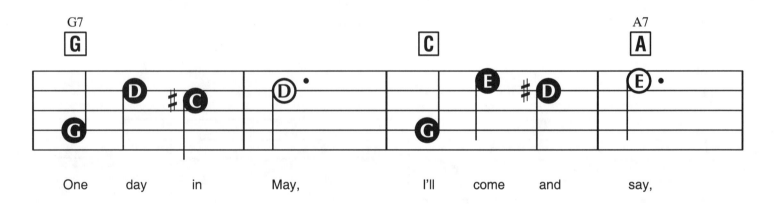

One day in May, I'll come and say,

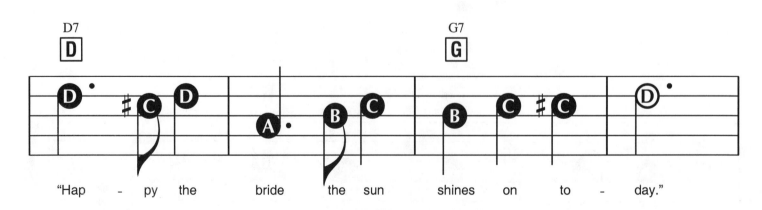

"Hap - py the bride the sun shines on to - day."

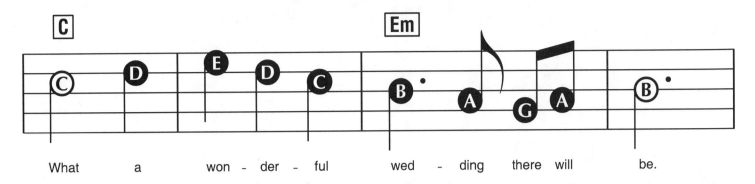

What a won - der - ful wed - ding there will be.

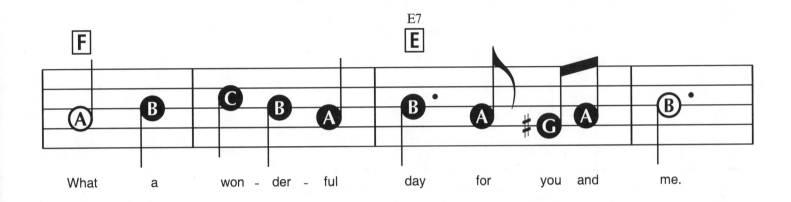

What a won - der - ful day for you and me.

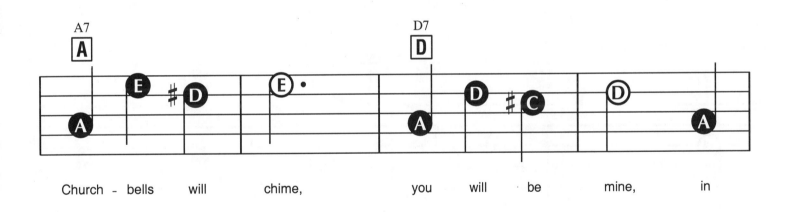

Church - bells will chime, you will be mine, in

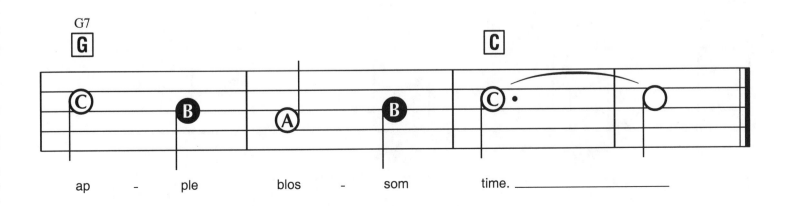

ap - ple blos - som time. _____

If I Had My Way

Registration 2
Rhythm: Waltz

Words by Lou Klein
Music by James Kendis

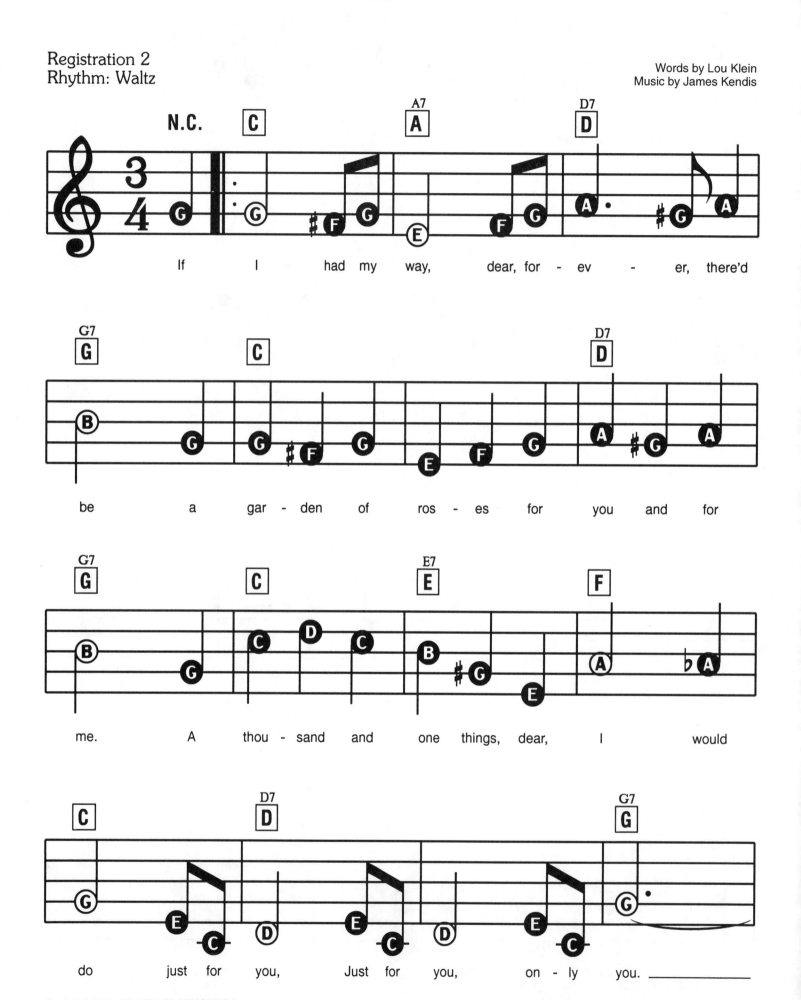

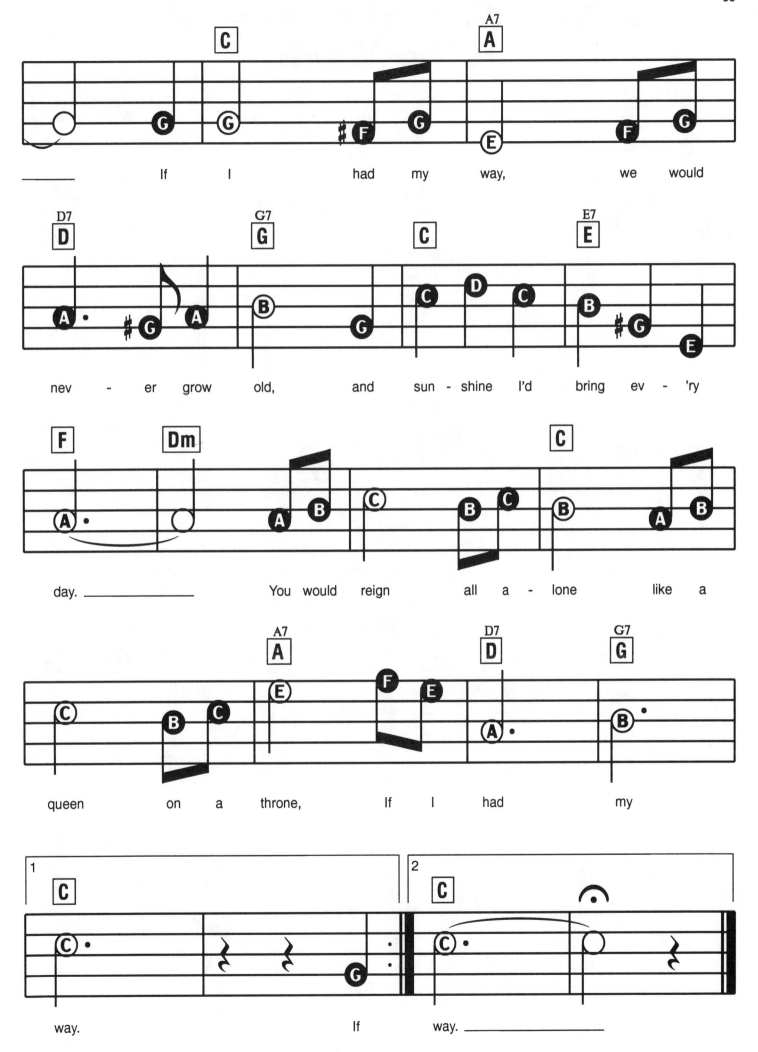

If You Were the Only Girl in the World

Registration 10
Rhythm: Waltz

Words by Clifford Grey
Music by Nat D. Ayer

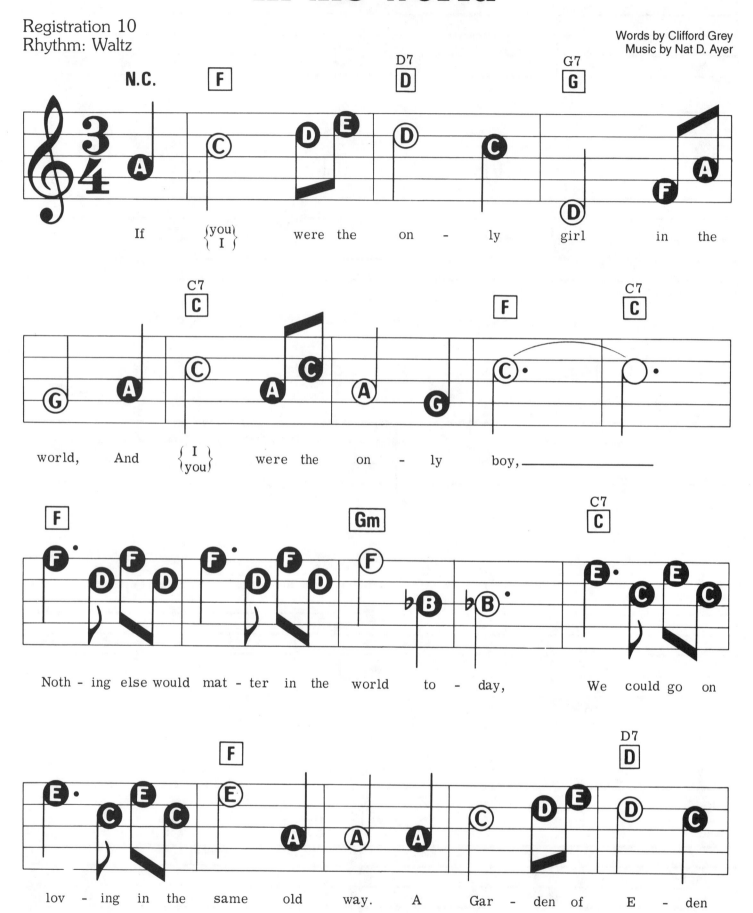

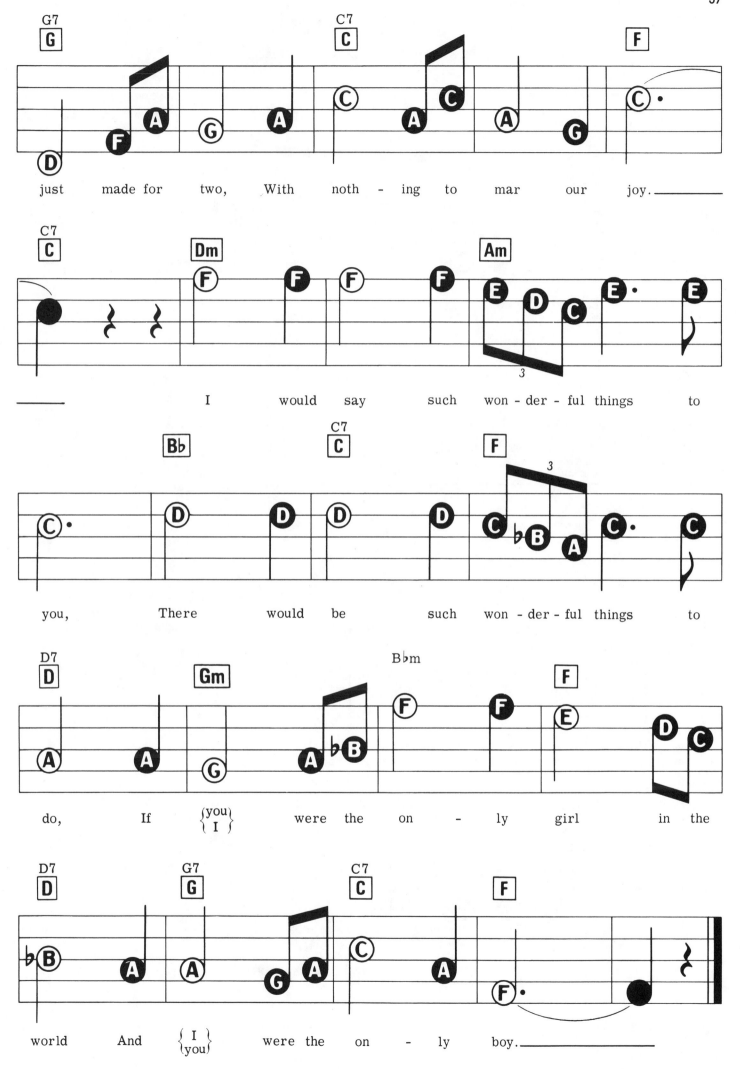

Indiana
(Back Home Again in Indiana)

Registration 3
Rhythm: Swing

Words by Ballard MacDonald
Music by James F. Hanley

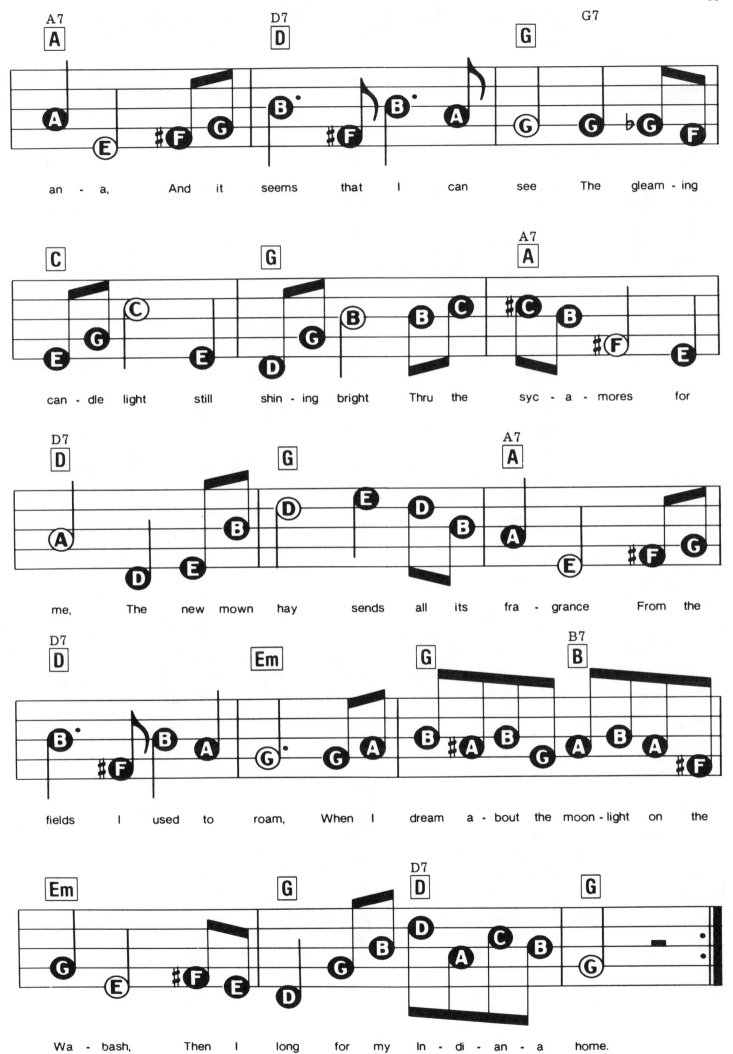

Let Me Call You Sweetheart

Registration 3
Rhythm: Waltz

Words by Beth Slater Whitson
Music by Leo Friedman

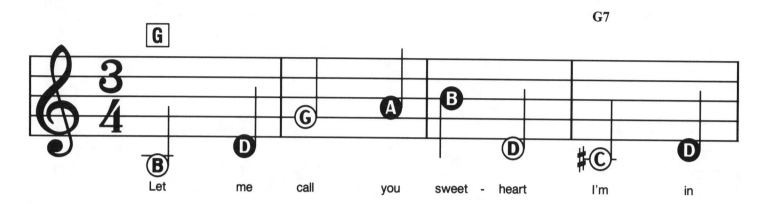

Let me call you sweet - heart I'm in

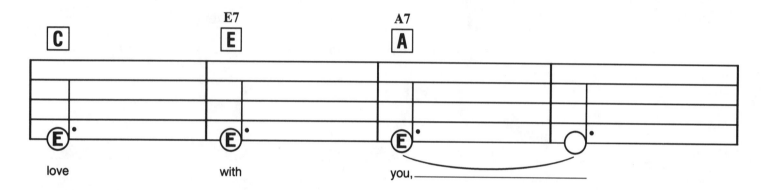

love with you,____

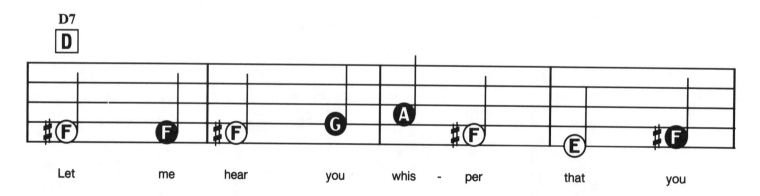

Let me hear you whis - per that you

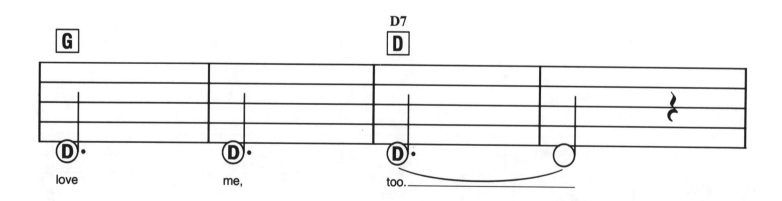

love me, too.____

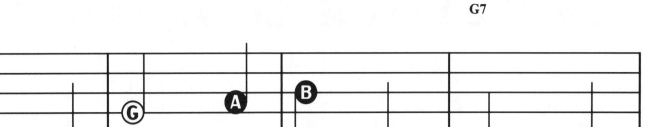

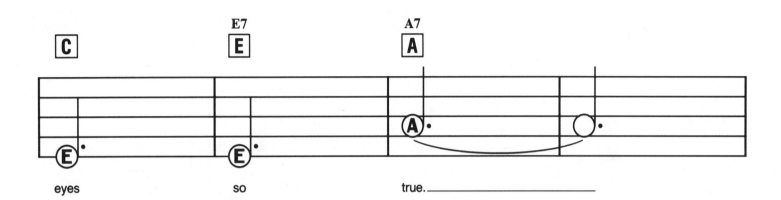

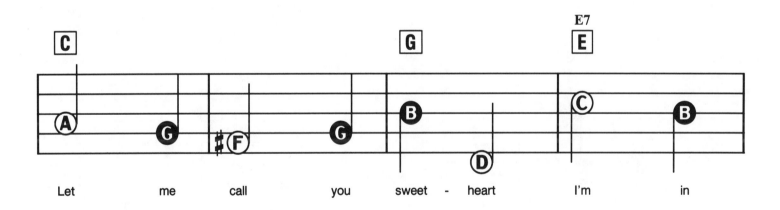

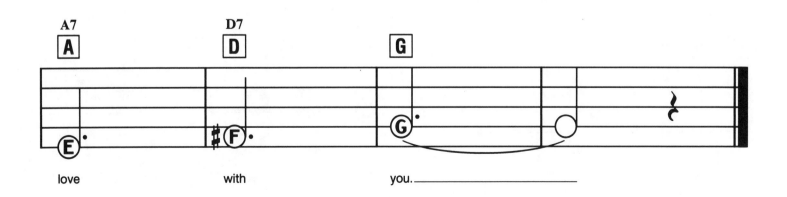

Let the Rest of the World Go By

Registration 5
Rhythm: Waltz

Words by J. Keirn Brennan
Music by Ernest R. Ball

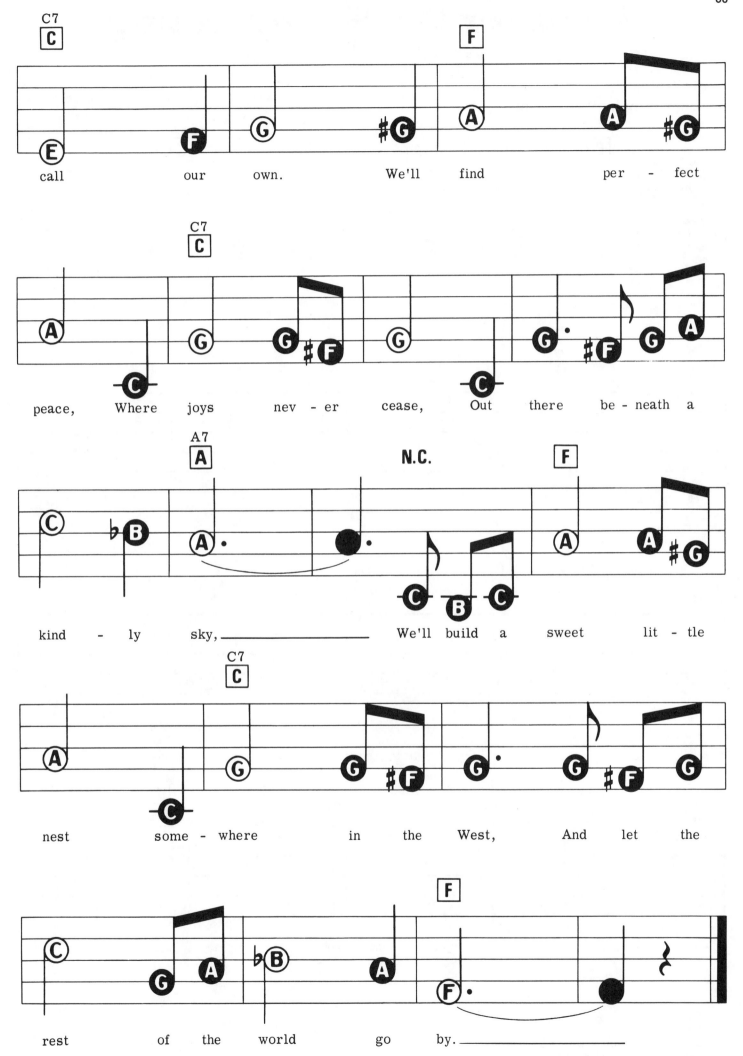

Look for the Silver Lining
from SALLY

Registration 2
Rhythm: Fox Trot or Swing

Words by Buddy DeSylva
Music by Jerome Kern

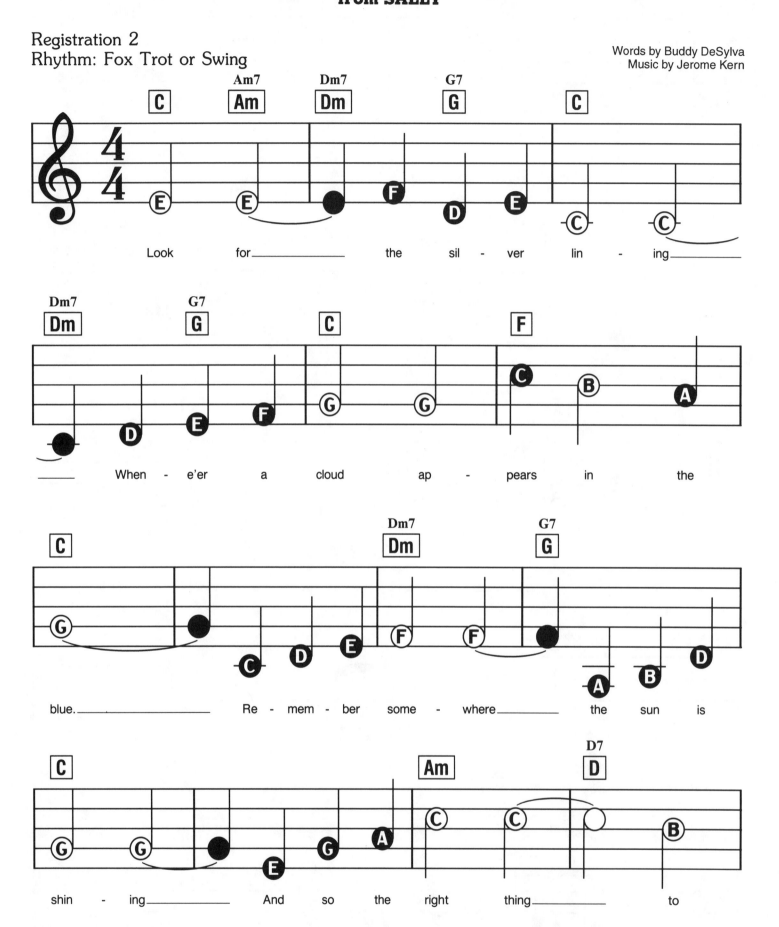

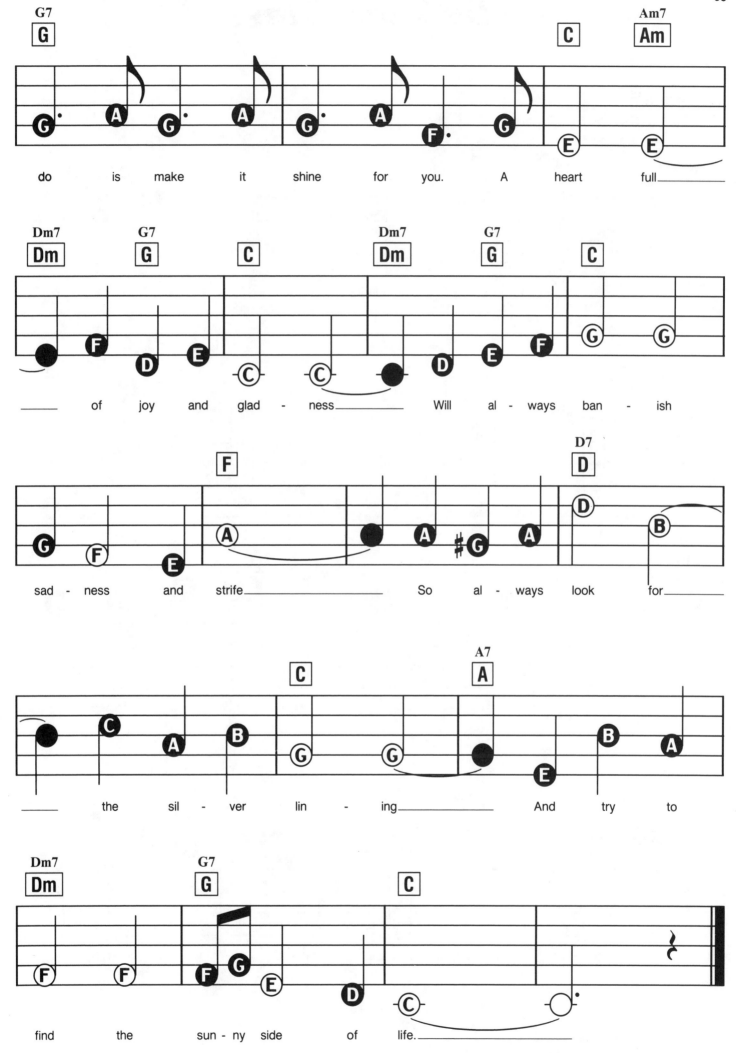

The Love Nest

Registration 9
Rhythm: Fox Trot or Swing

Words by Otto Harbach
Music by Louis A. Hirsch

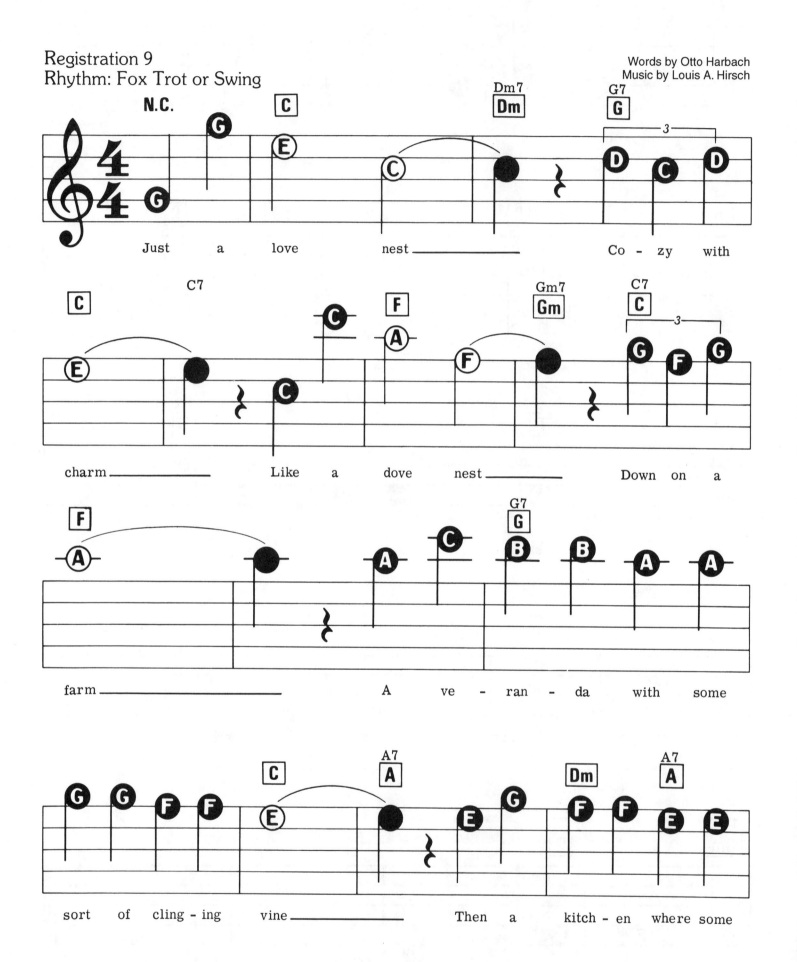

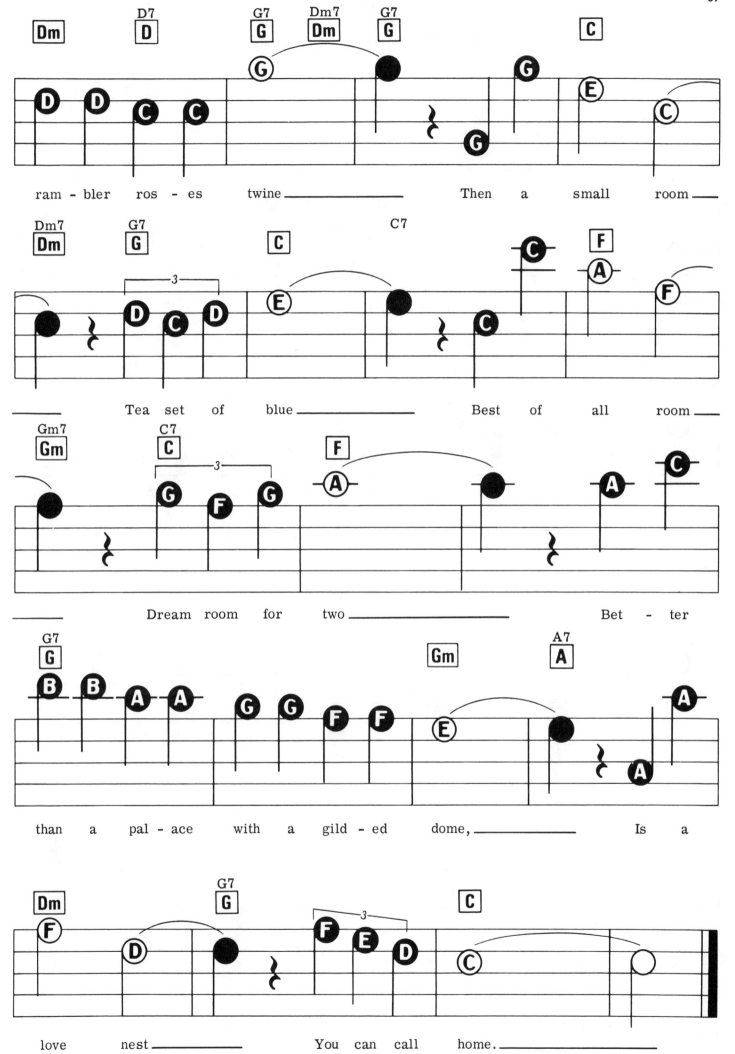

Ma
(He's Making Eyes at Me)

Registration 4
Rhythm: Swing

Words by Sidney Clare
Music by Con Conrad

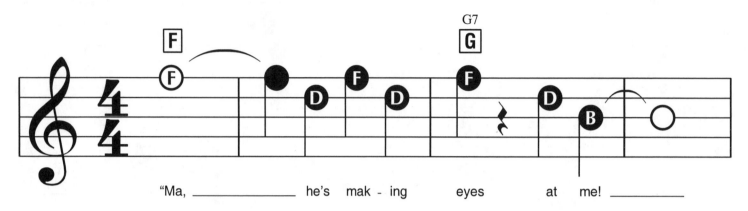

"Ma, _____ he's mak - ing eyes at me! _____

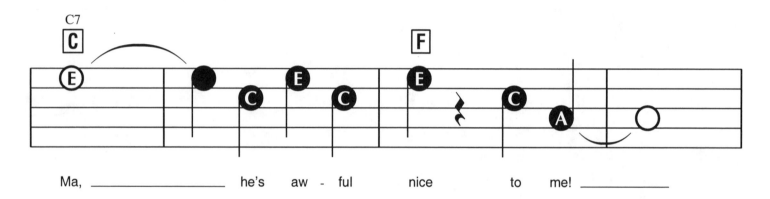

Ma, _____ he's aw - ful nice to me! _____

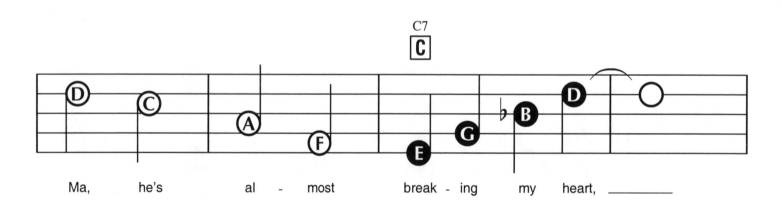

Ma, he's al - most break - ing my heart, _____

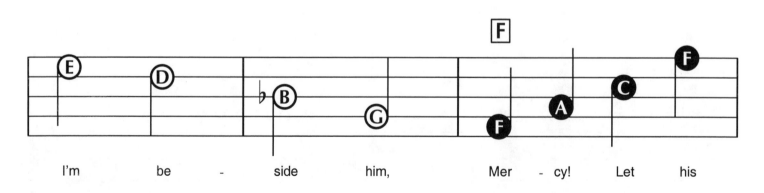

I'm be - side him, Mer - cy! Let his

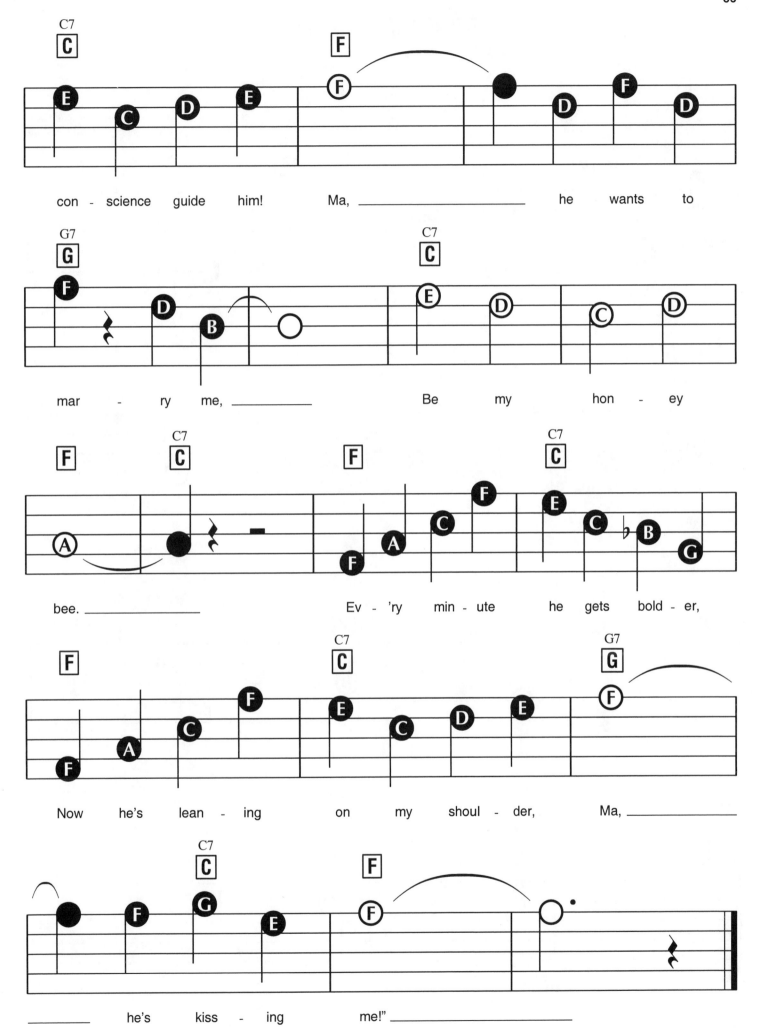

Memories

Registration 3
Rhythm: Waltz

Words by Gus Kahn
Music by Egbert Van Alstyne

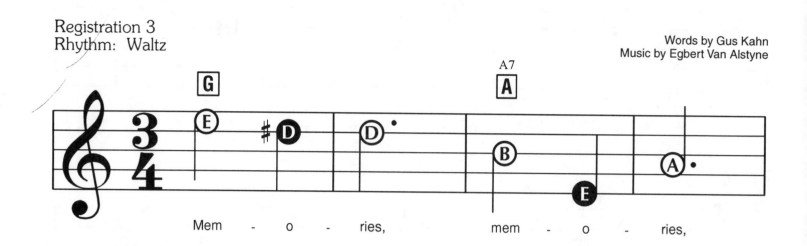

Mem - o - ries, mem - o - ries,

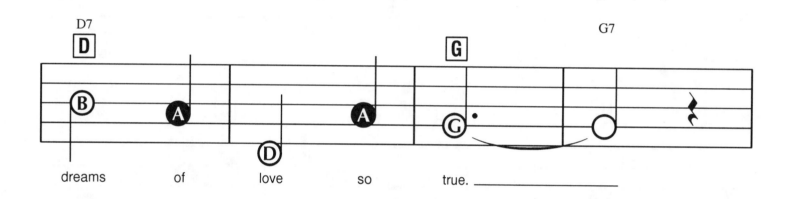

dreams of love so true. _____

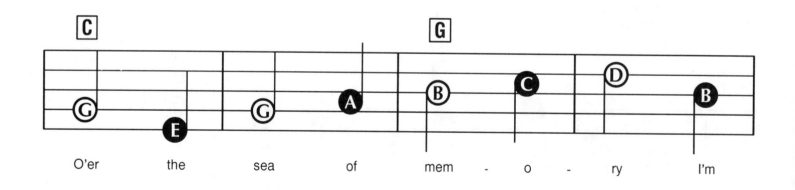

O'er the sea of mem - o - ry I'm

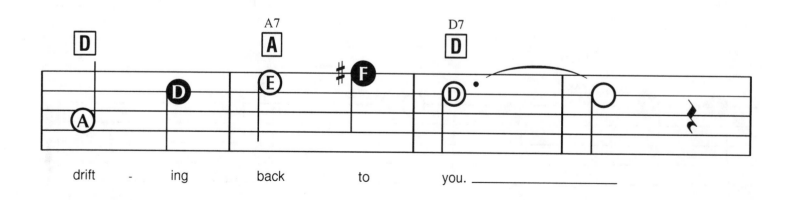

drift - ing back to you. _____

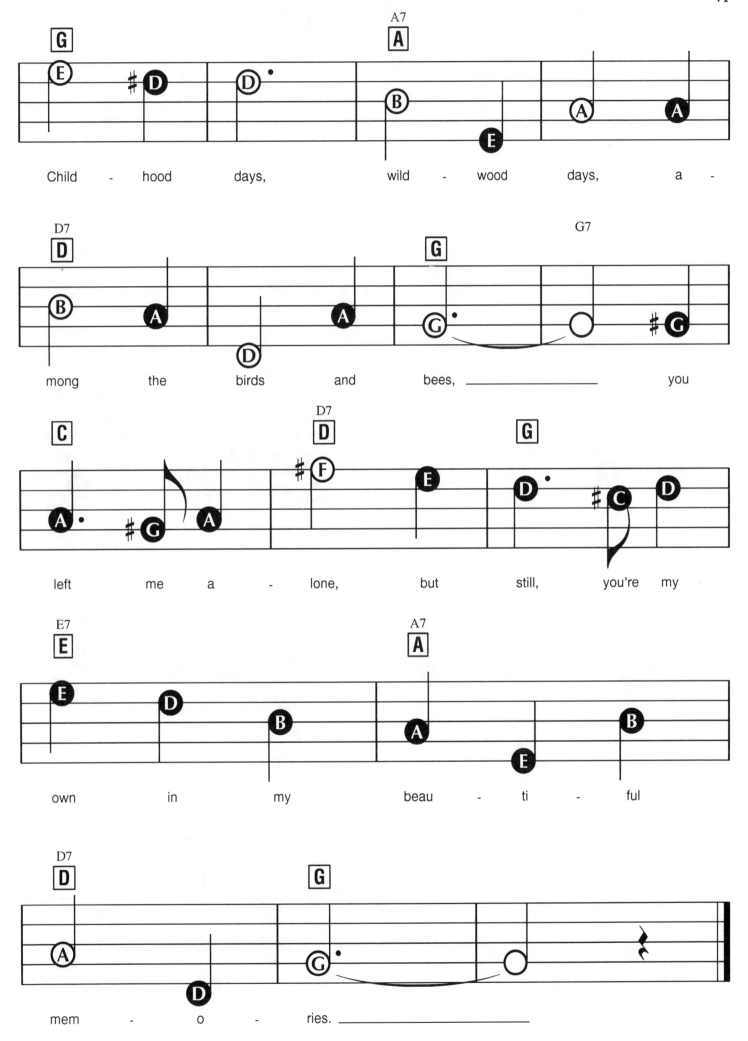

My Buddy

Registration 9
Rhythm: Waltz

Lyrics by Gus Kahn
Music by Walter Donaldson

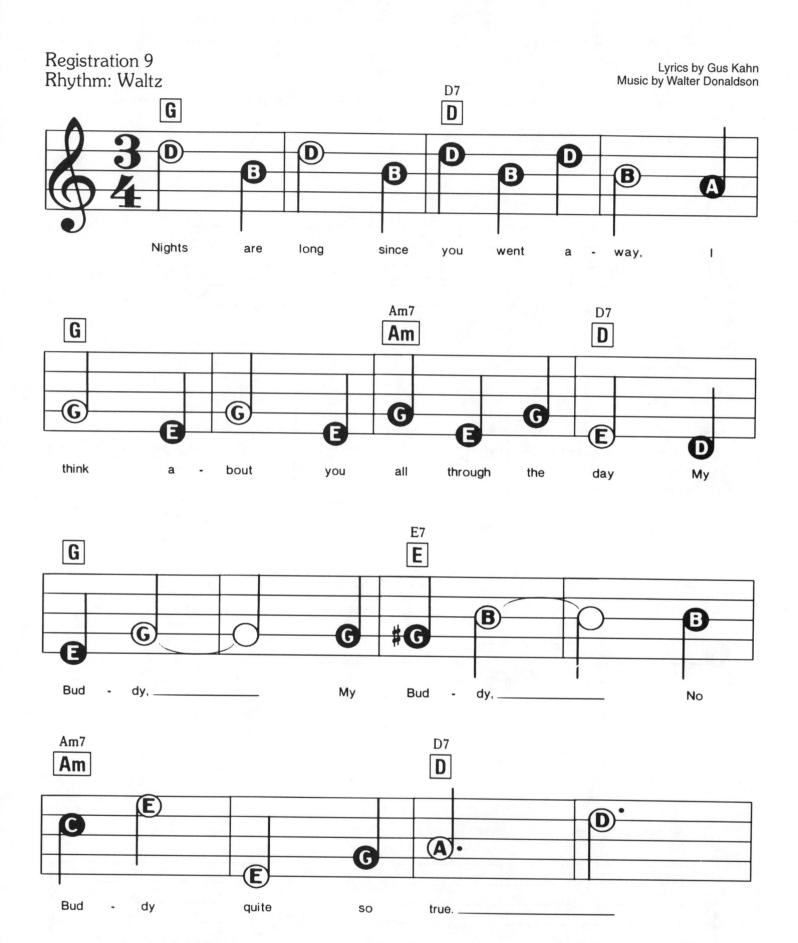

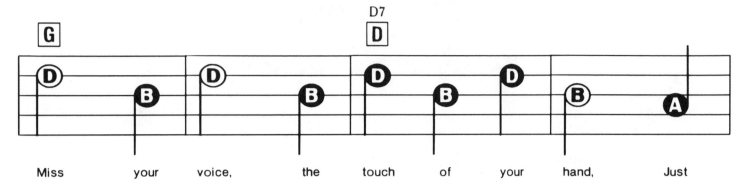

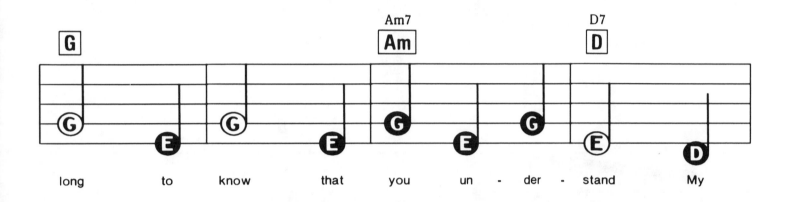

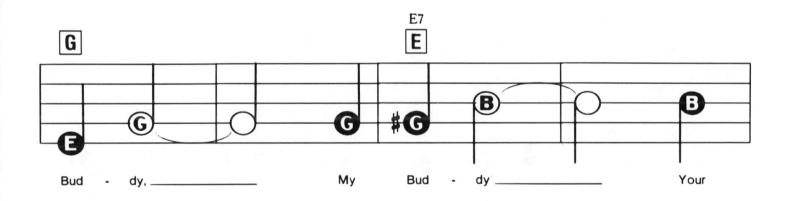

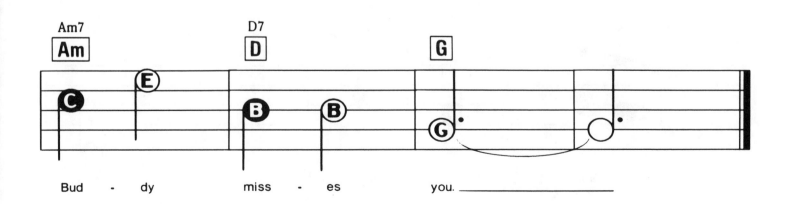

My Man
(Mon Homme)
from ZIEGFELD FOLLIES

Registration 2
Rhythm: Fox Trot

Words by Albert Willemetz and Jacques Charles
English Words by Channing Pollock
Music by Maurice Yvain

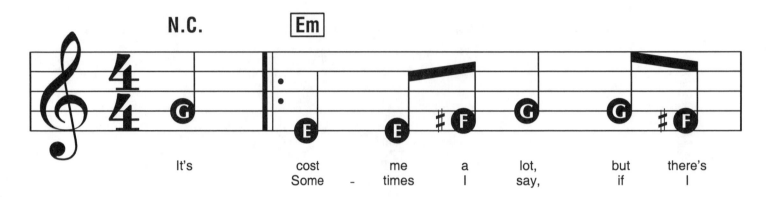

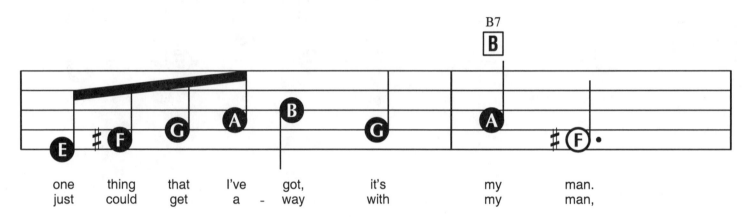

It's cost me a lot, but there's
Some - times I say, if I

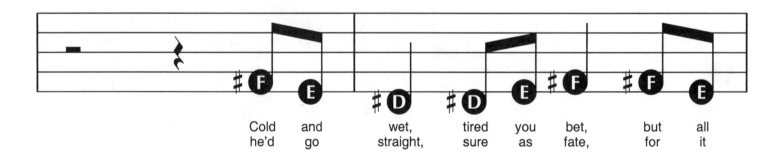

one thing that I've got, it's my man.
just could that get a - way with my man,

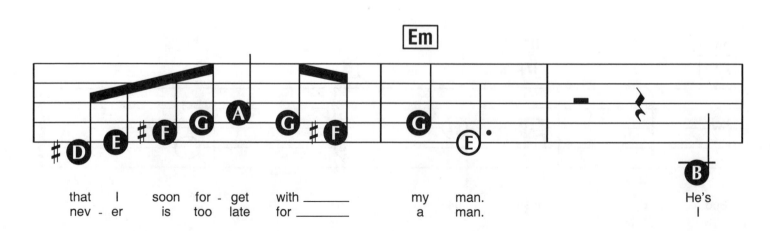

Cold and wet, tired you bet, but all
he'd go straight, sure as fate, but for it

that I soon for - get with _____ my man.
nev - er is too late for _____ a man.

He's
I

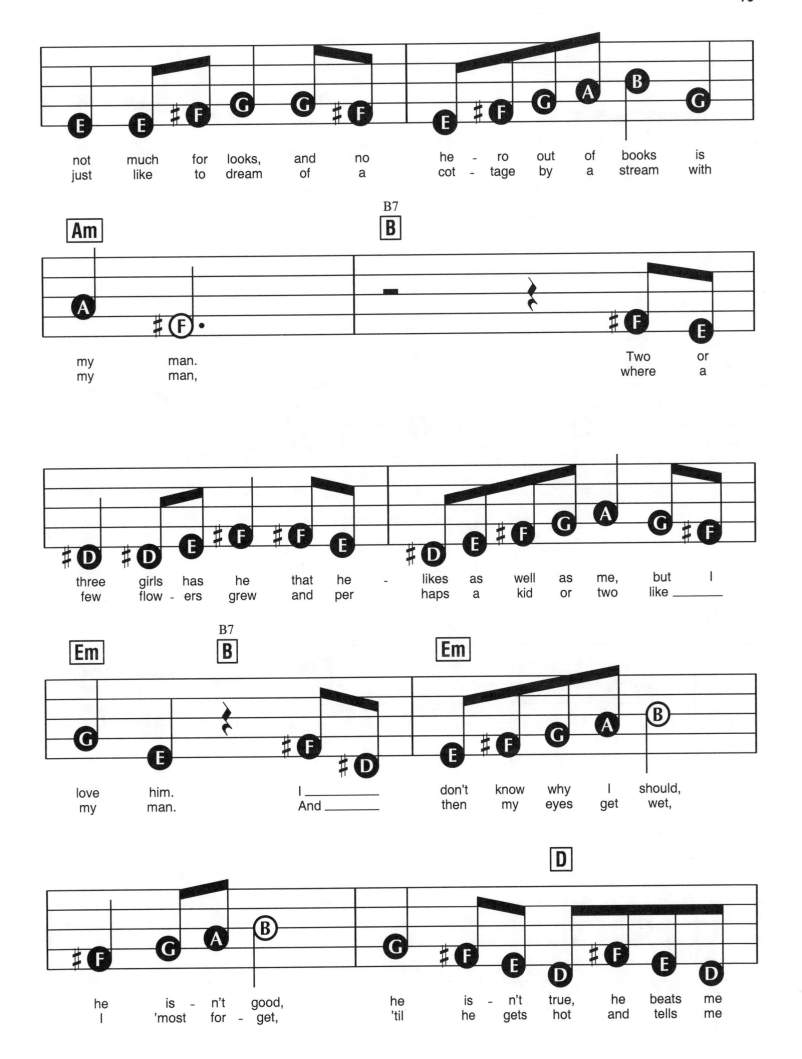

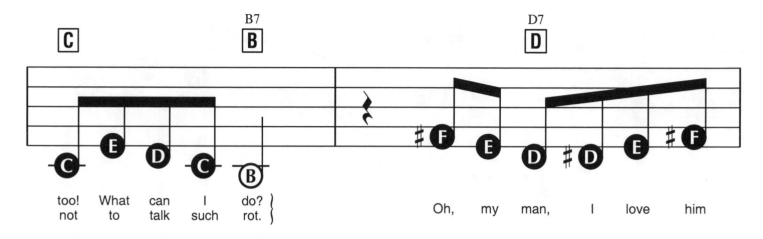

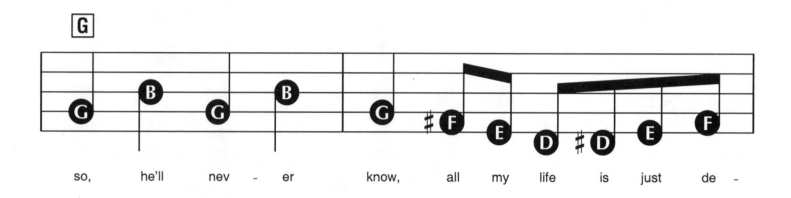

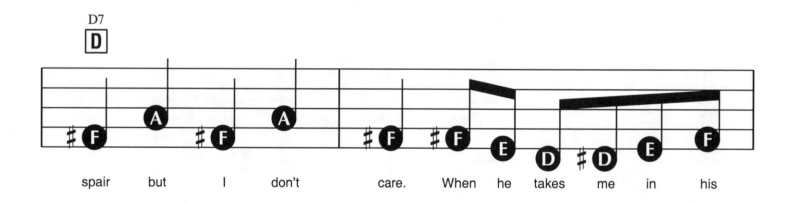

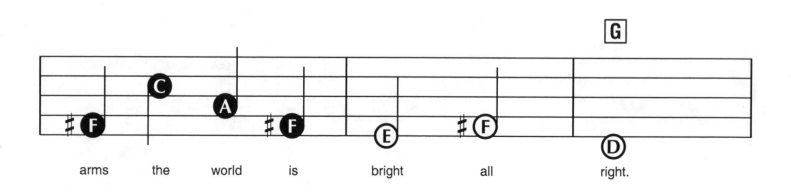

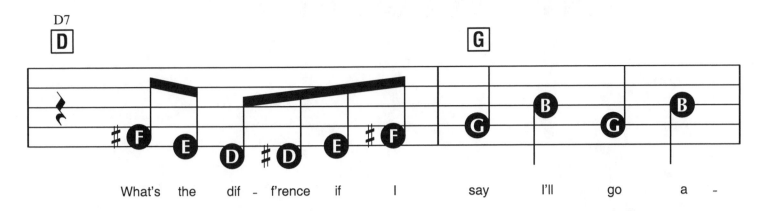

What's the dif – f'rence if I say I'll go a –

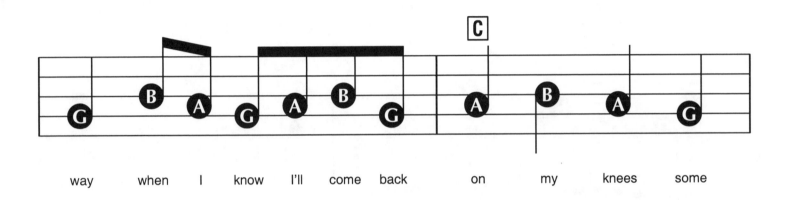

way when I know I'll come back on my knees some

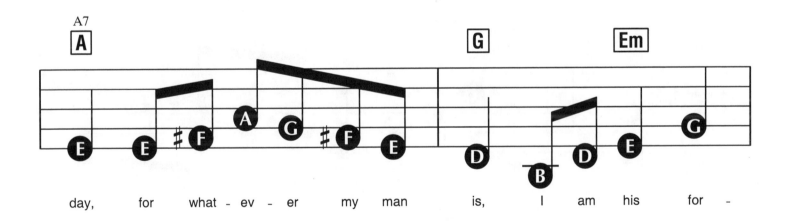

day, for what – ev – er my man is, I am his for –

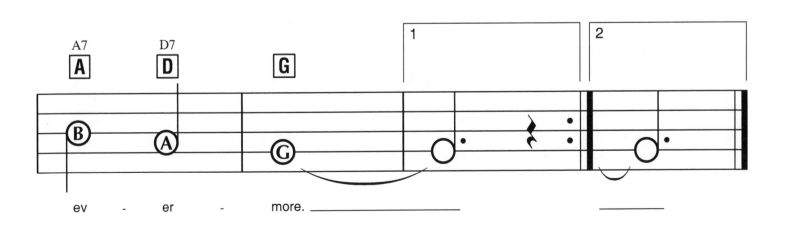

ev – er – more.

My Melancholy Baby

Registration 3
Rhythm: Swing

Words by George Norton
Music by Ernie Burnett

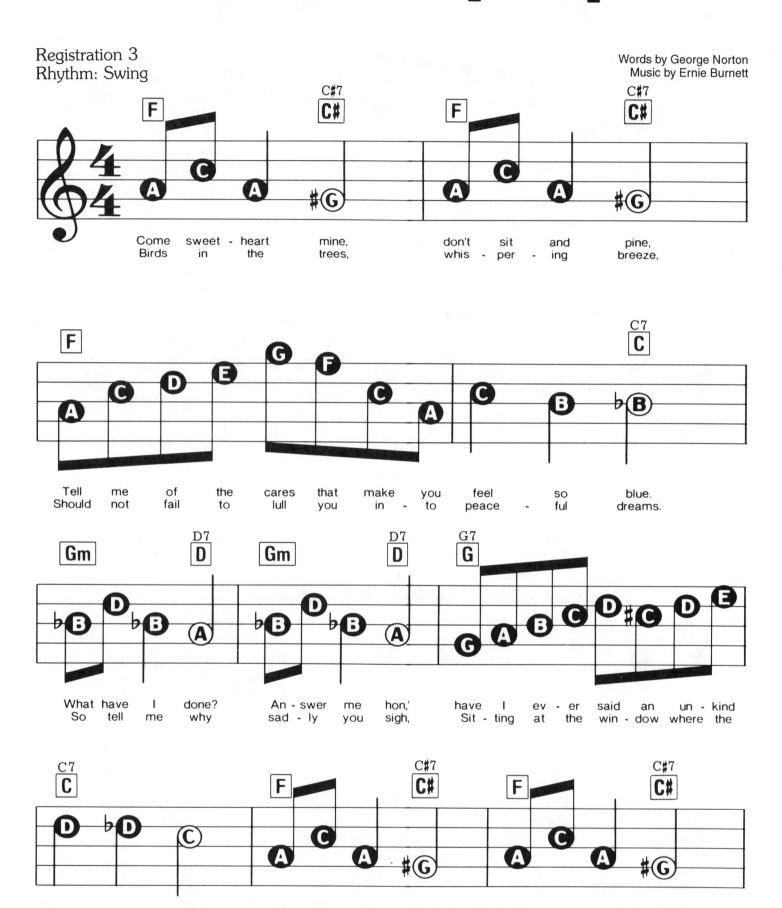

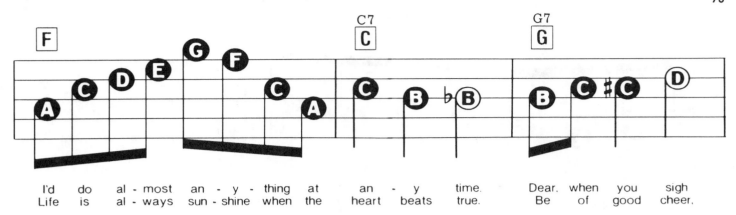

I'd do al - most an - y - thing at an - y time. Dear, when you sigh
Life is al - ways sun - shine when the heart beats true. Be of good cheer,

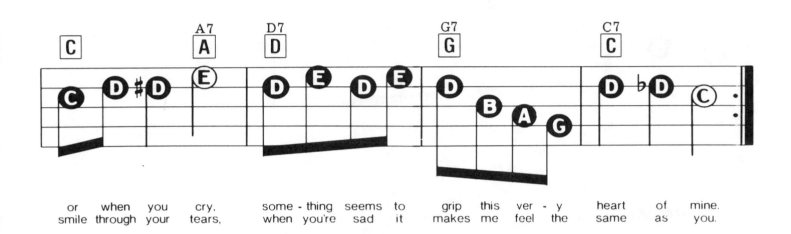

or when you cry, some - thing seems to grip this ver - y heart of mine.
smile through your tears, when you're sad it makes me feel the same as you.

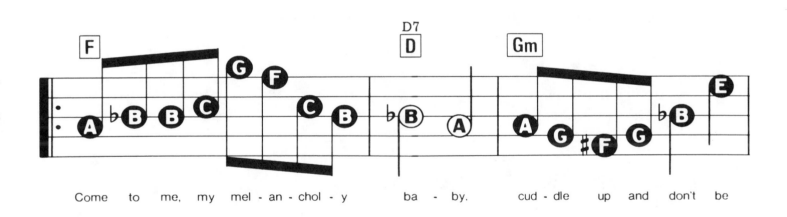

Come to me, my mel - an - chol - y ba - by, cud - dle up and don't be

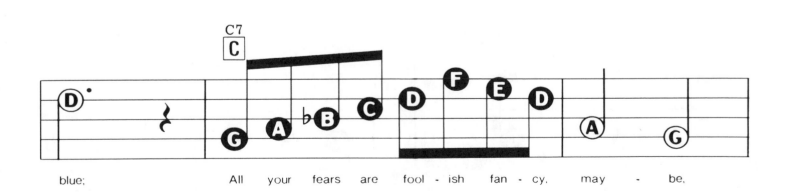

blue; All your fears are fool - ish fan - cy, may - be,

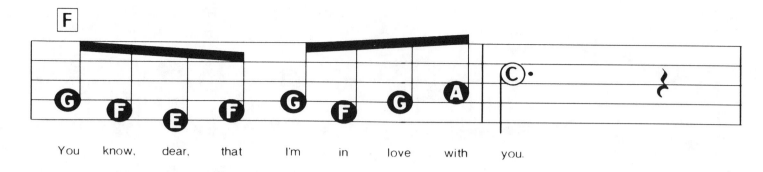

You know, dear, that I'm in love with you.

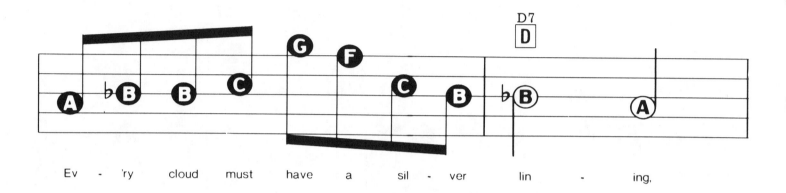

Ev - 'ry cloud must have a sil - ver lin - ing,

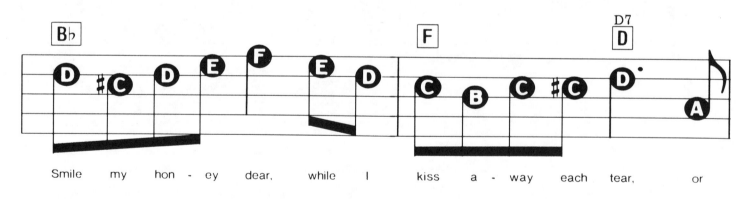

wait un - til the sun shines through.

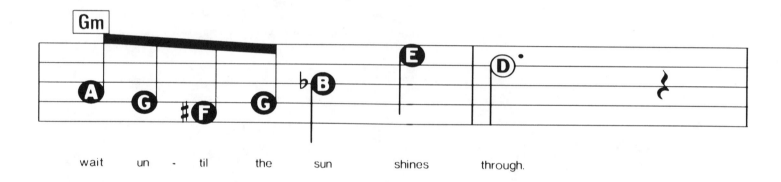

Smile my hon - ey dear, while I kiss a - way each tear, or

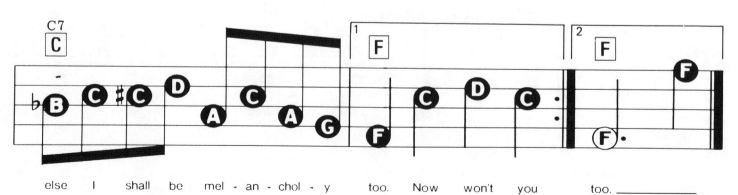

else I shall be mel - an - chol - y too. Now won't you too. _____

Oh Johnny, Oh Johnny, Oh!

Registration 7
Rhythm: Polka

Words by Ed Rose
Music by Abe Olman

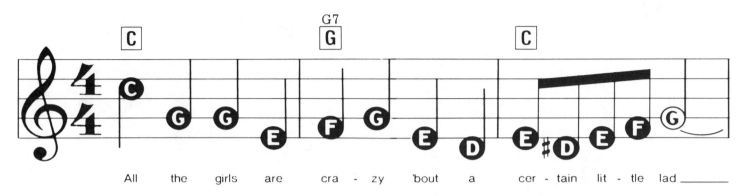

All the girls are cra - zy 'bout a cer - tain lit - tle lad _____

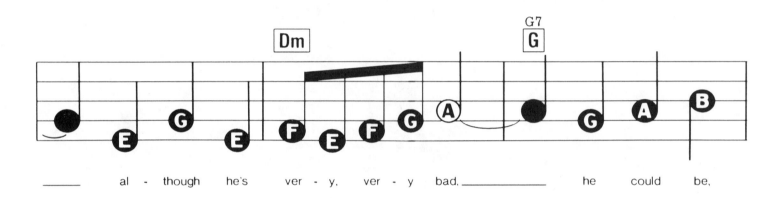

_____ al - though he's ver - y, ver - y bad, _____ he could be,

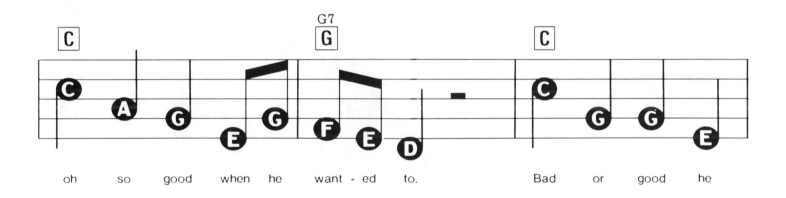

oh so good when he want - ed to, Bad or good he

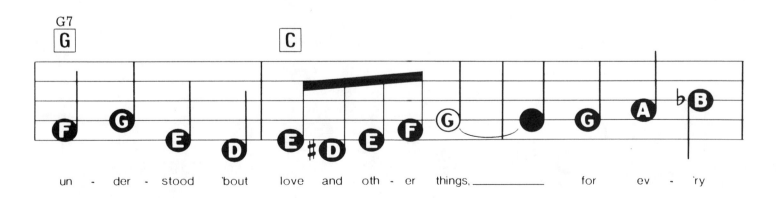

un - der - stood 'bout love and oth - er things, _____ for ev - 'ry

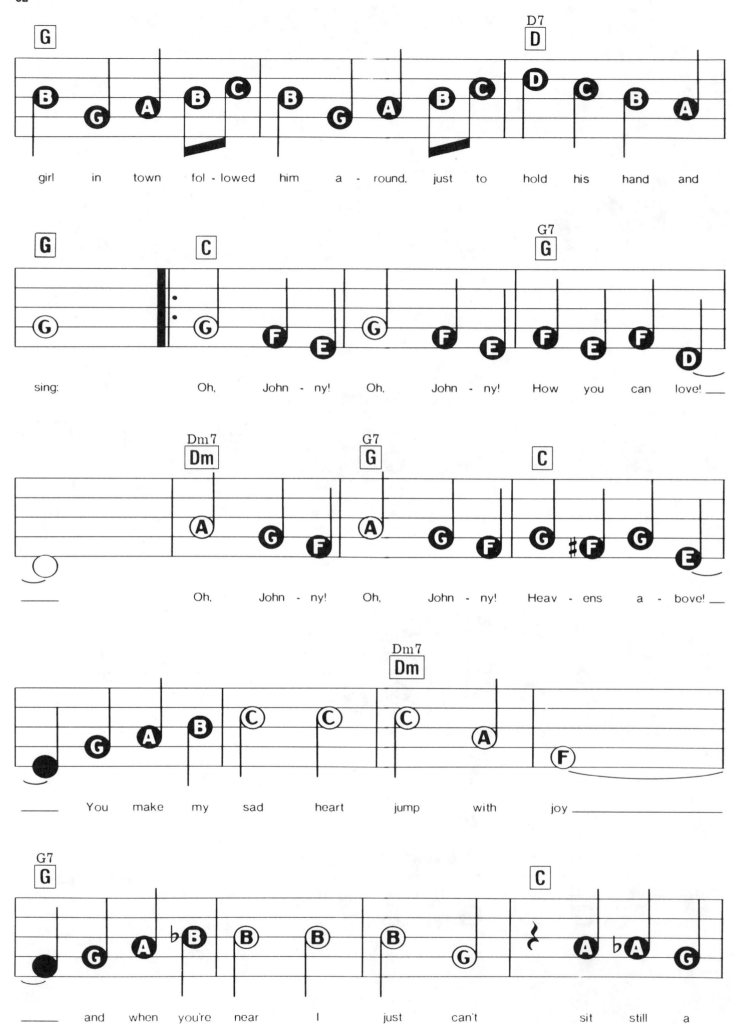

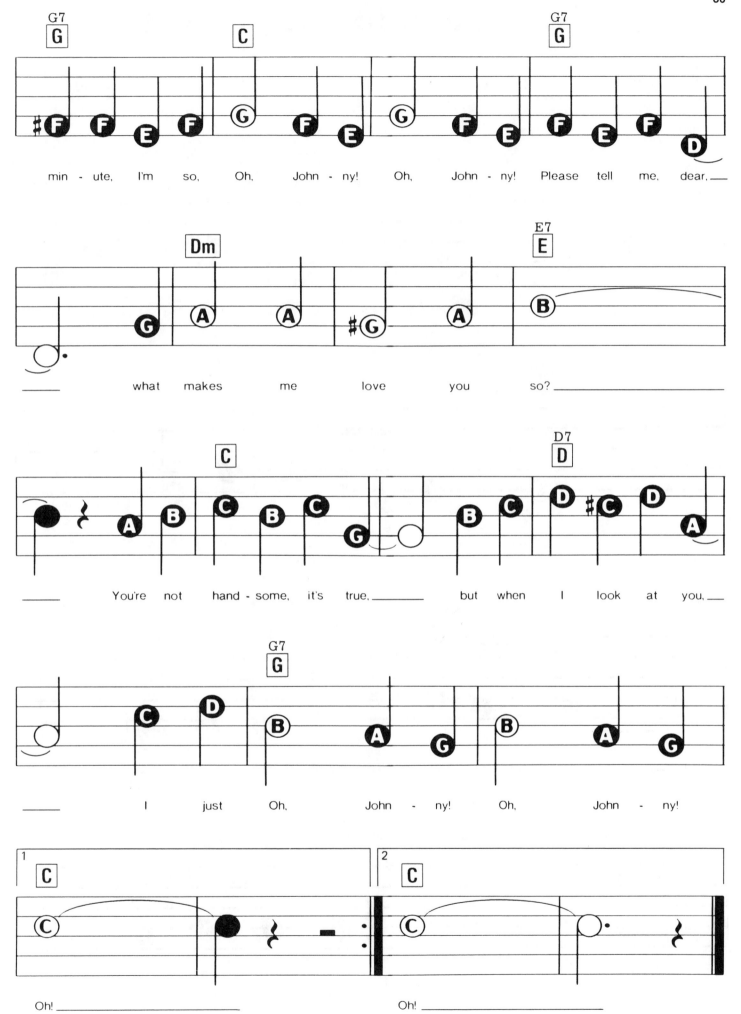

Oh! You Beautiful Doll

Registration 3
Rhythm: Fox Trot or Swing

Words by A. Seymour Brown
Music by Nat D. Ayer

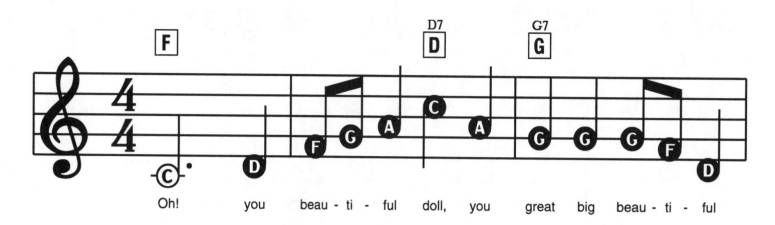

Oh! you beau - ti - ful doll, you great big beau - ti - ful

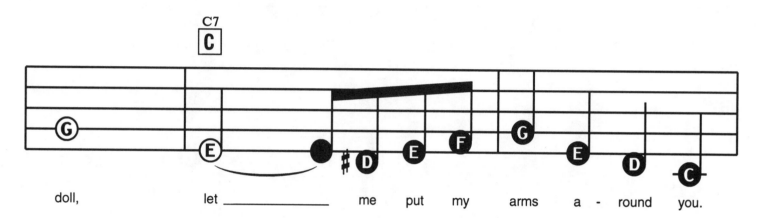

doll, let _____ me put my arms a - round you.

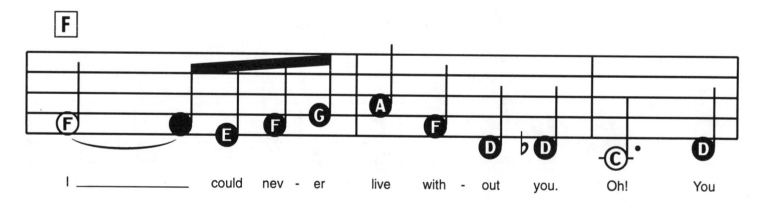

I _____ could nev - er live with - out you. Oh! You

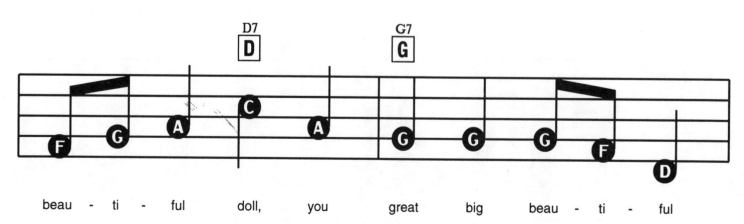

beau - ti - ful doll, you great big beau - ti - ful

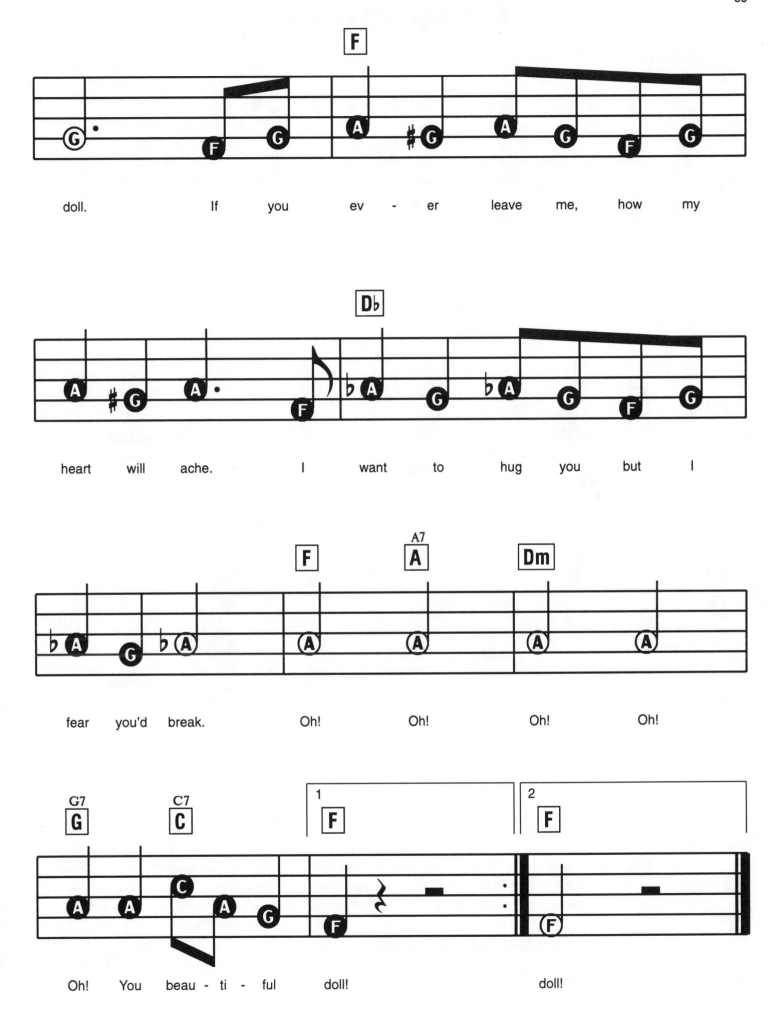

doll.   If   you   ev - er   leave   me,   how   my

heart   will   ache.   I   want   to   hug   you   but   I

fear   you'd   break.   Oh!   Oh!   Oh!   Oh!

Oh!   You   beau - ti - ful   doll!   doll!

Over There

Registration 9
Rhythm: March

Words and Music by
George M. Cohan

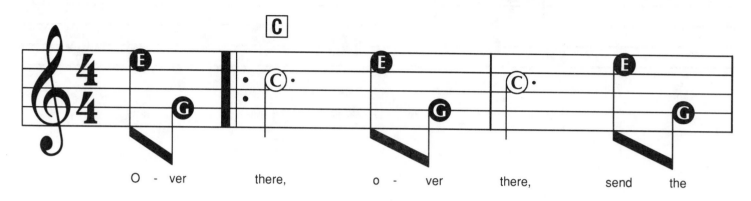

O - ver there, o - ver there, send the

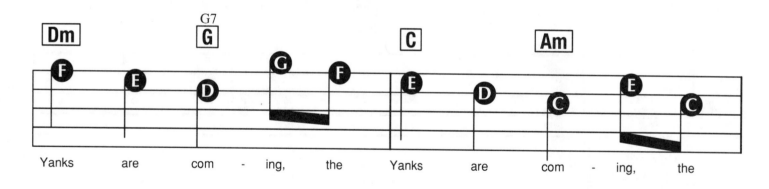

word, send the word o - ver there that the

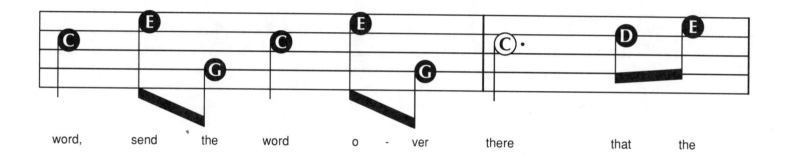

Yanks are com - ing, the Yanks are com - ing, the

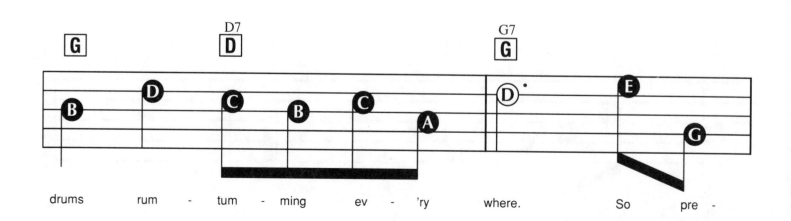

drums rum - tum - ming ev - 'ry where. So pre -

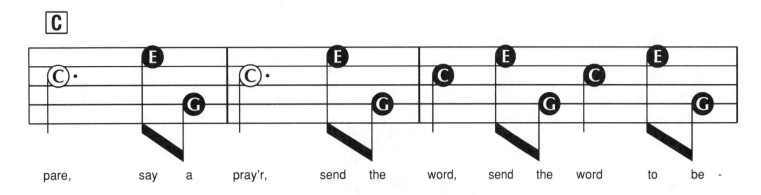

pare, say a pray'r, send the word, send the word to be -

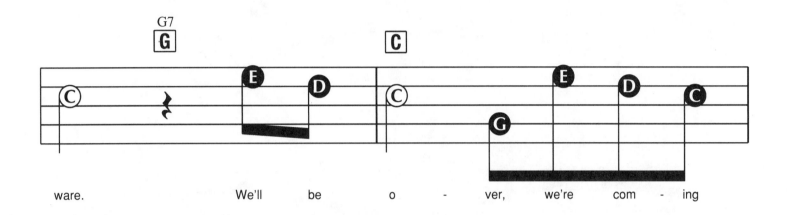

ware. We'll be o - ver, we're com - ing

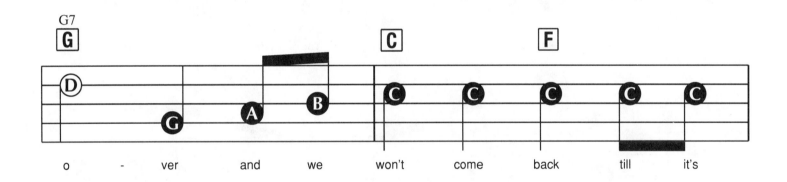

o - ver and we won't come back till it's

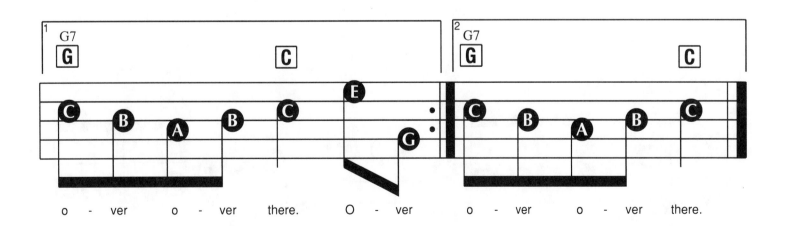

o - ver o - ver there. O - ver o - ver o - ver there.

Paper Doll

Registration 4
Rhythm: Fox Trot or Swing

Words and Music by
Johnny S. Black

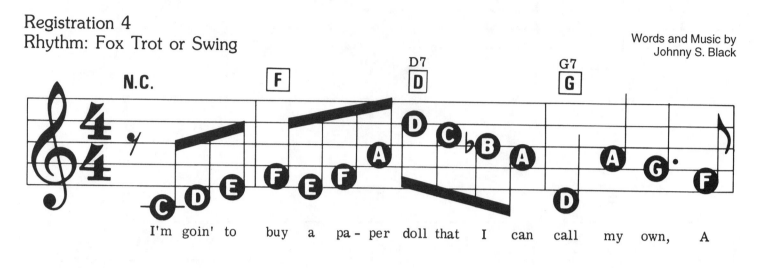

I'm goin' to buy a pa-per doll that I can call my own, A

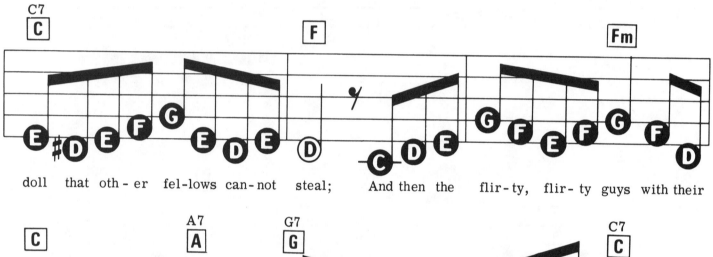

doll that oth-er fel-lows can-not steal; And then the flir-ty, flir-ty guys with their

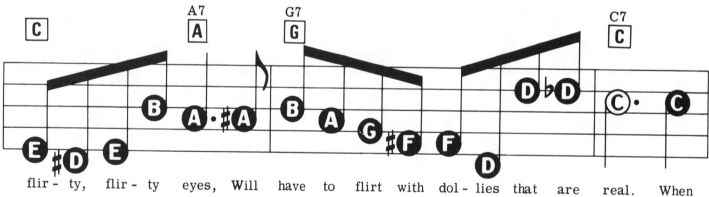

flir-ty, flir-ty eyes, Will have to flirt with dol-lies that are real. When

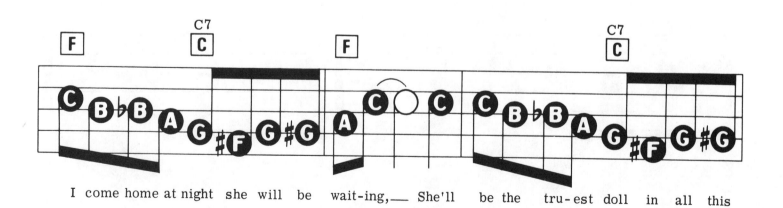

I come home at night she will be wait-ing,— She'll be the tru-est doll in all this

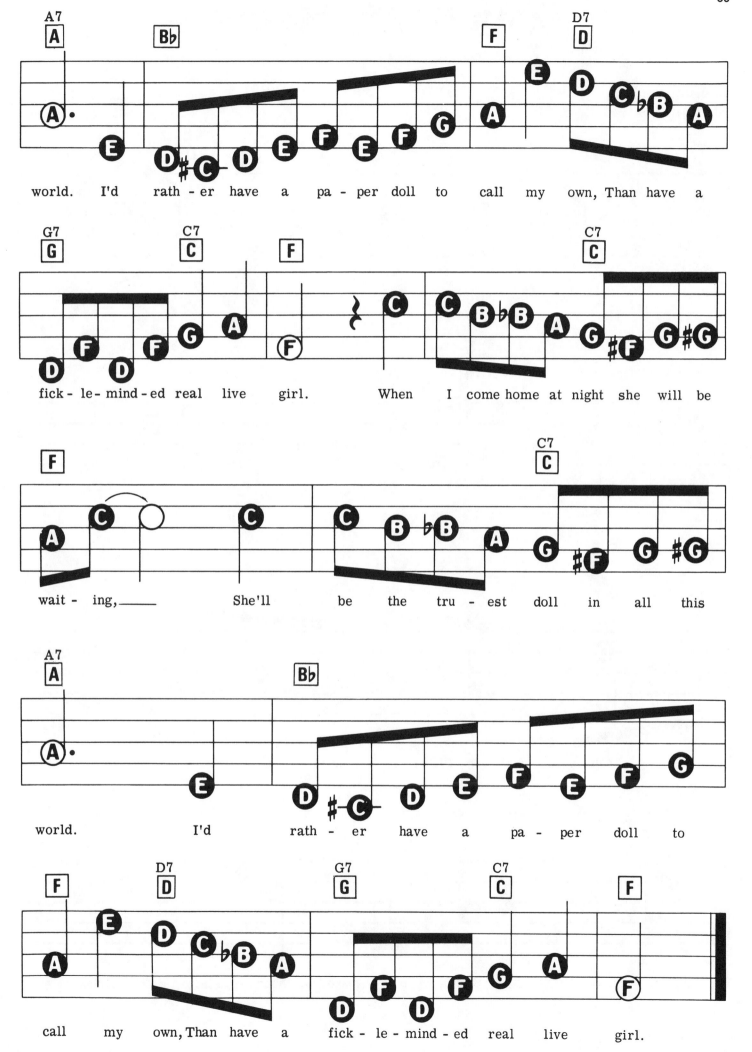

Peg O' My Heart

Registration 2
Rhythm: Fox Trot or Swing

Words by Alfred Bryan
Music by Fred Fisher

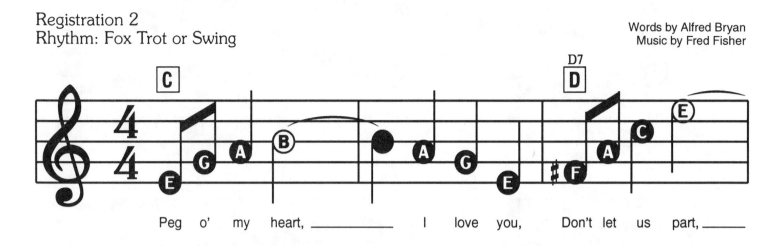

Peg o' my heart, _____ I love you, Don't let us part, _____

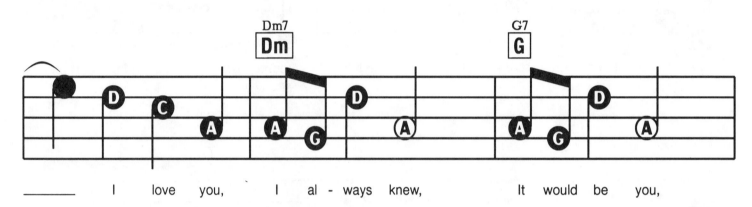

_____ I love you, I al - ways knew, It would be you,

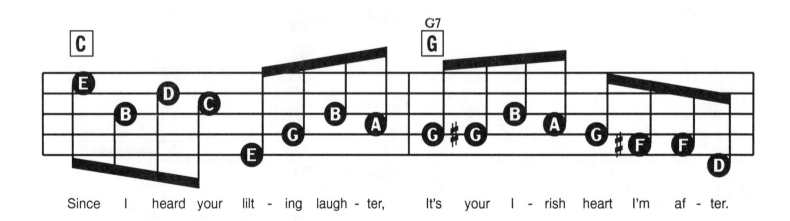

Since I heard your lilt - ing laugh - ter, It's your I - rish heart I'm af - ter.

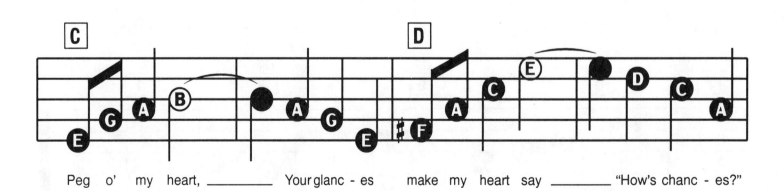

Peg o' my heart, _____ Your glanc - es make my heart say _____ "How's chanc - es?"

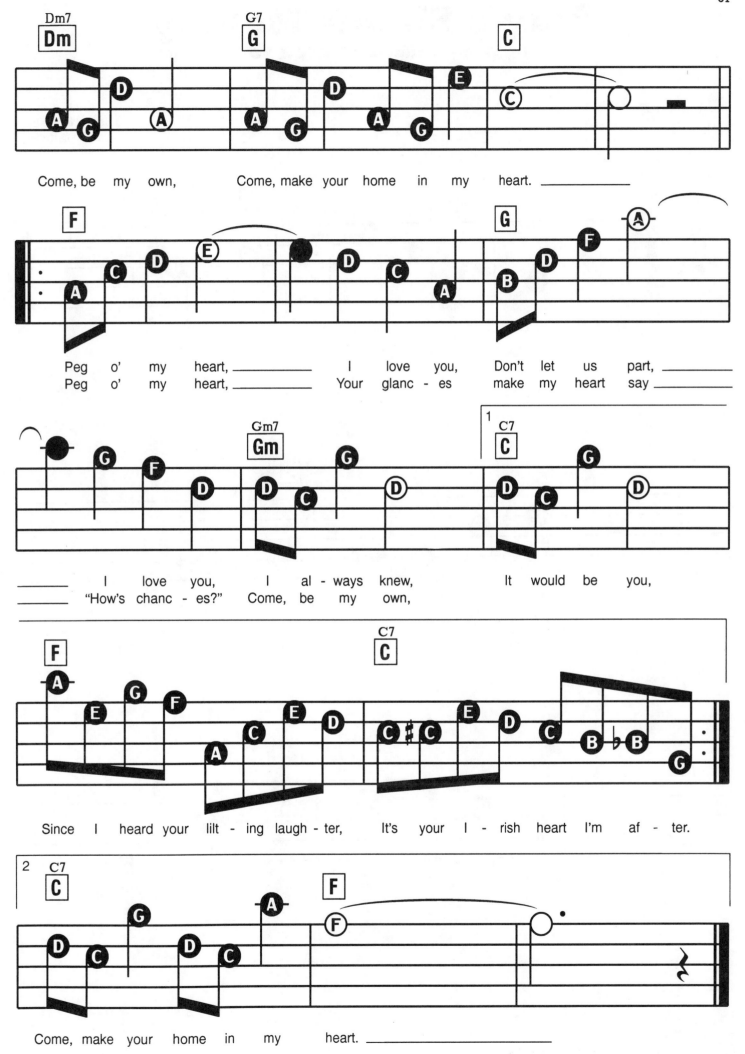

Play a Simple Melody
from the Stage Production WATCH YOUR STEP

Registration 1
Rhythm: Swing

Words and Music by
Irving Berlin

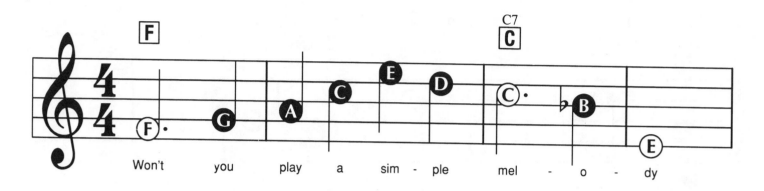

Won't you play a sim - ple mel - o - dy

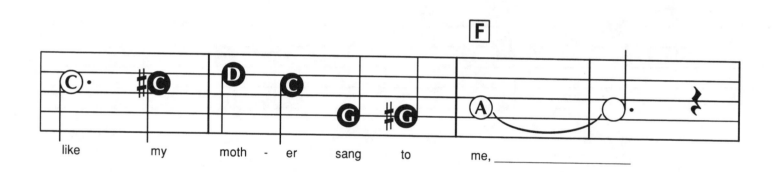

like my moth - er sang to me, _____

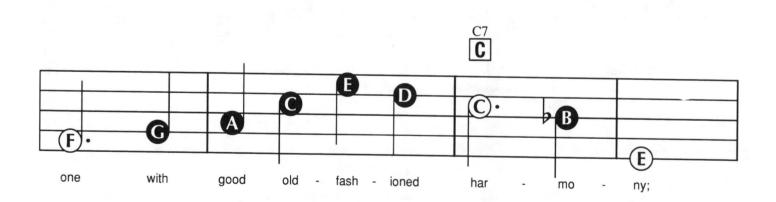

one with good old - fash - ioned har - mo - ny;

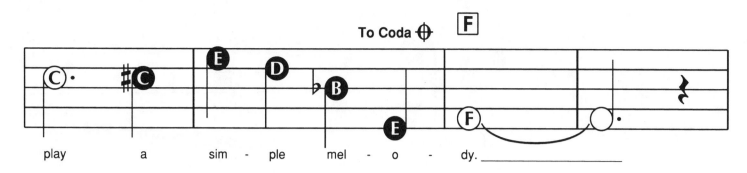

play a sim - ple mel - o - dy. _____

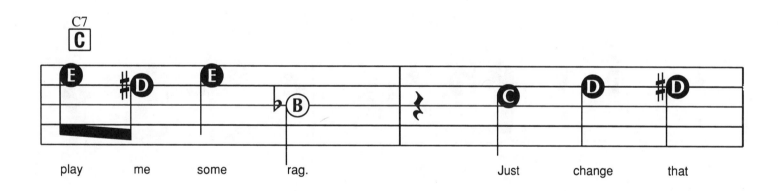

Mu - si - cal de - mon, set your hon - ey a - dream - in', won't you

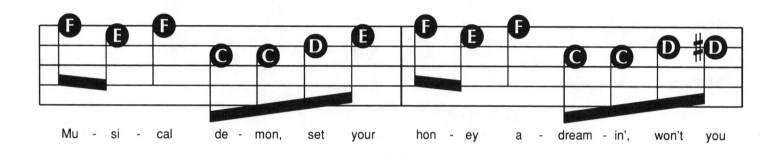

play me some rag. Just change that

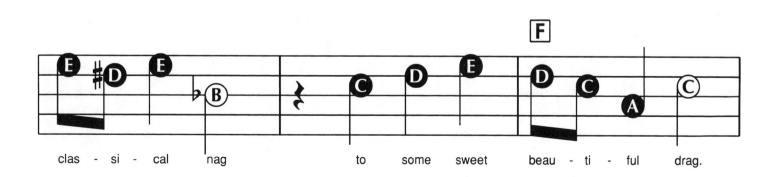

clas - si - cal nag to some sweet beau - ti - ful drag.

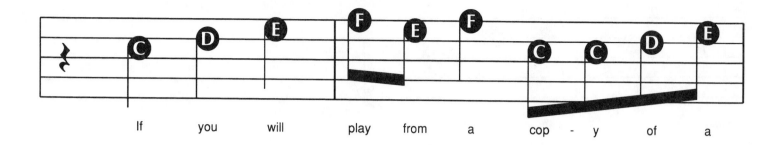

If you will play from a cop - y of a

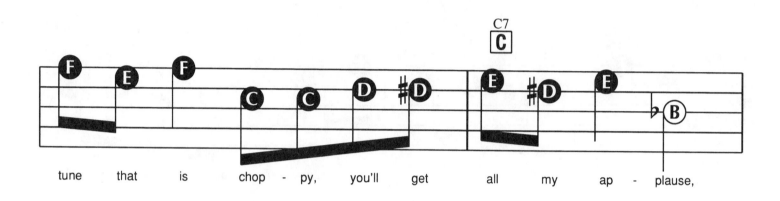

tune that is chop - py, you'll get all my ap - plause,

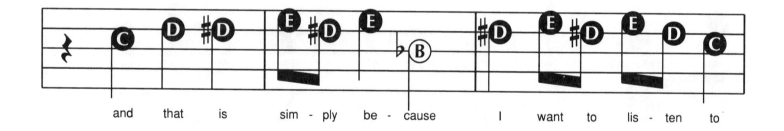

and that is sim - ply be - cause I want to lis - ten to

D.C. al Coda
(Return to beginning
Play to ⊕
Skip to Coda)

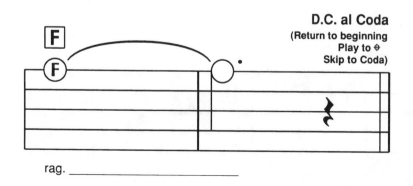

rag. _____

CODA F

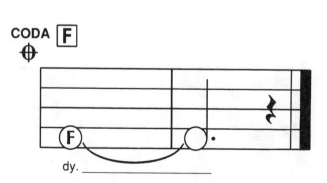

dy. _____

Rock-A-Bye Your Baby
with a Dixie Melody
from SINBAD

Registration 9
Rhythm: Fox Trot or Swing

Words by Sam M. Lewis and Joe Young
Music by Jean Schwartz

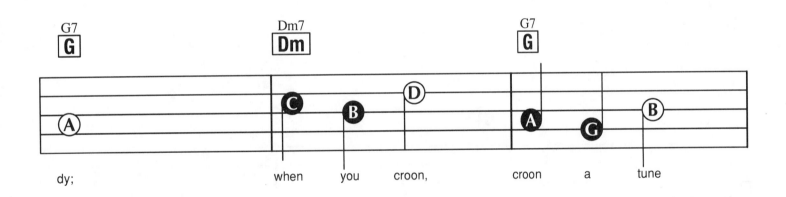

Rock - a - bye your ba - by with a Dix - ie mel - o -

dy;   when   you   croon,   croon   a   tune

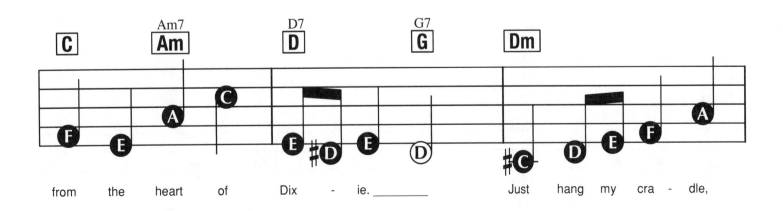

from   the   heart   of   Dix - ie. _____   Just   hang   my   cra - dle,

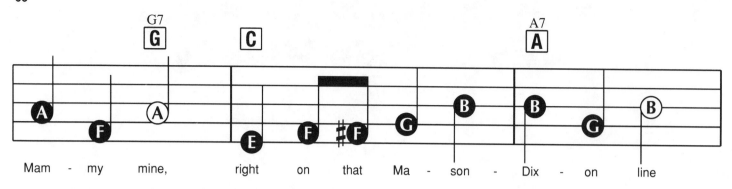

Mam - my mine, right on that Ma - son - Dix - on line

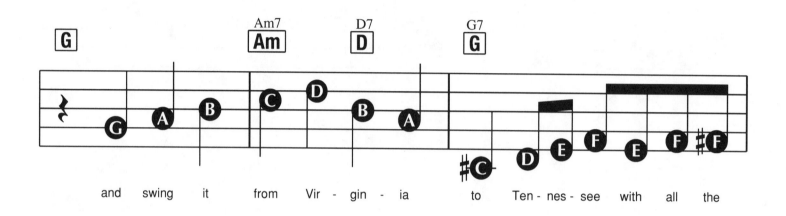

and swing it from Vir - gin - ia to Ten - nes - see with all the

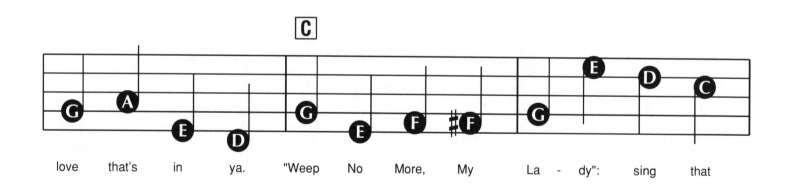

love that's in ya. "Weep No More, My La - dy": sing that

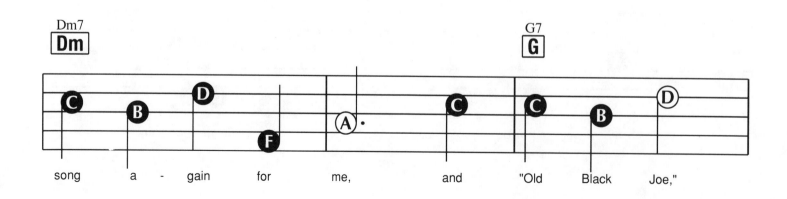

song a - gain for me, and "Old Black Joe,"

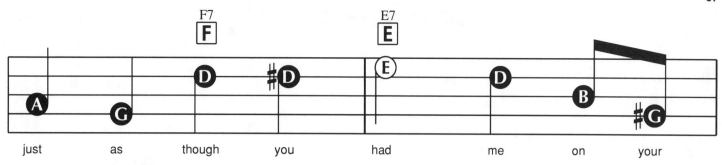

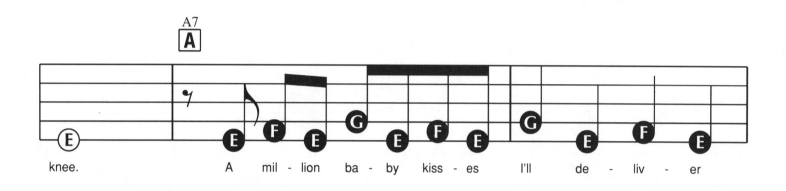

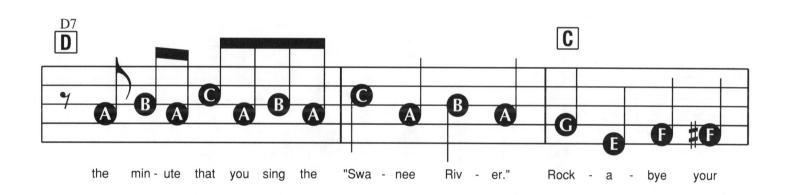

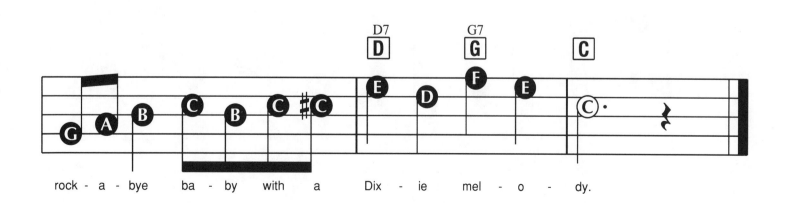

Poor Butterfly

Registration 1
Rhythm: Fox Trot or Swing

Words by John L. Golden
Music by Raymond Hubbell

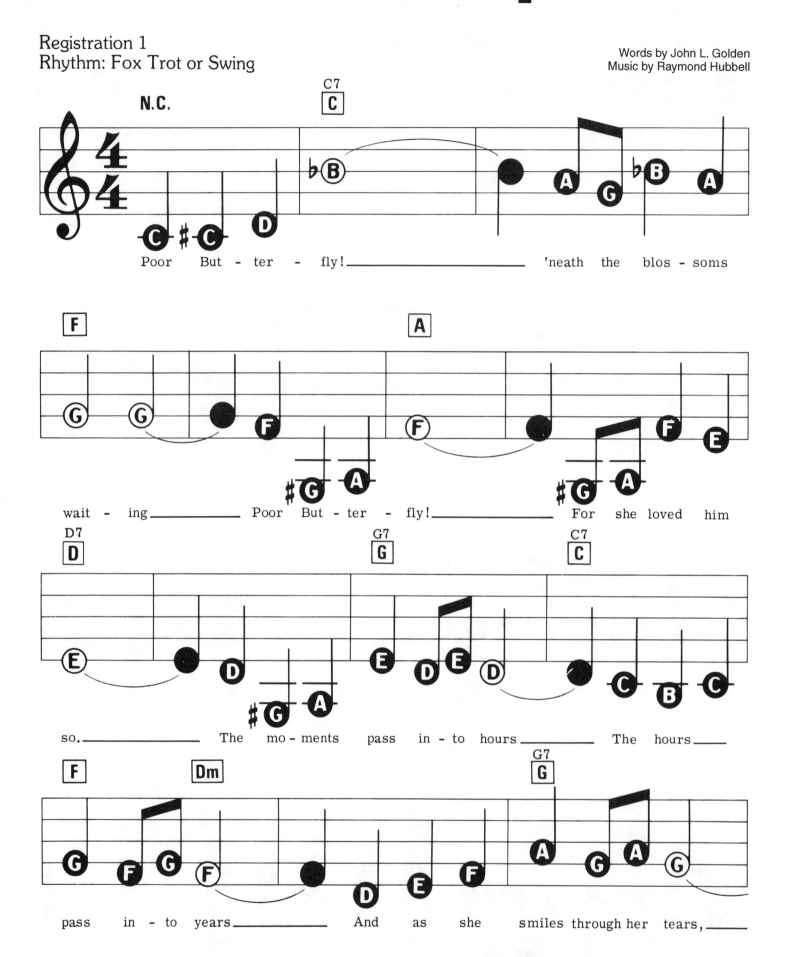

99

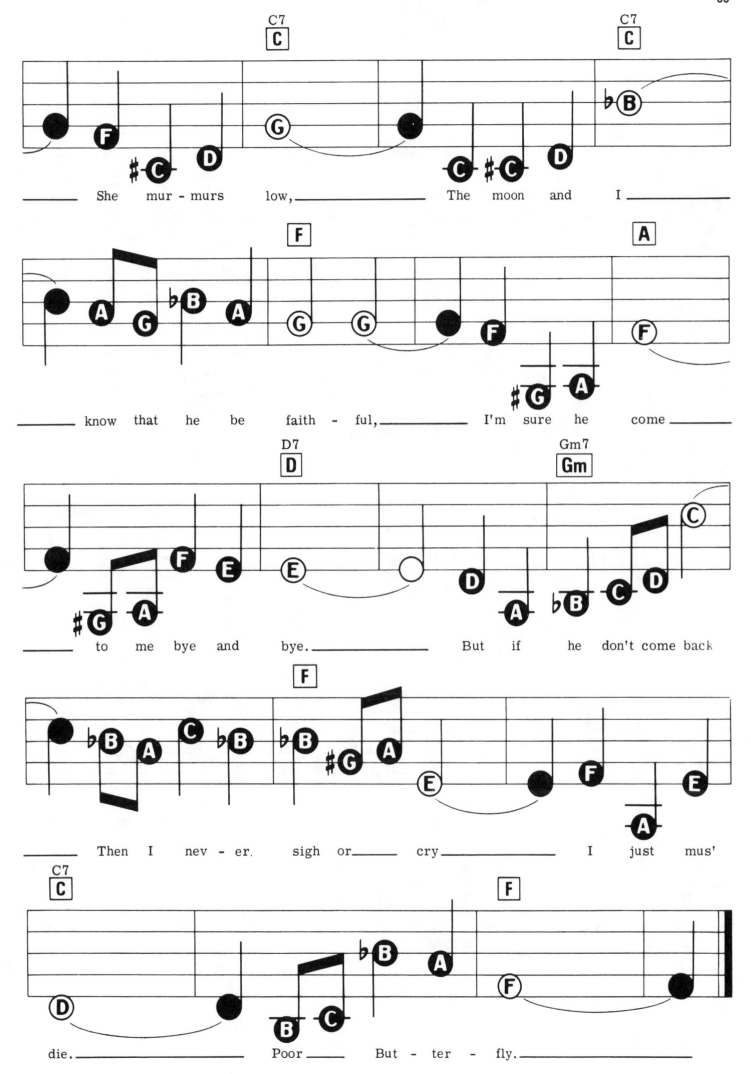

Pretty Baby

Registration 2
Rhythm: Swing

Words by Gus Kahn
Music by Egbert Van Alstyne and Tony Jackson

You ask me why I'm al - ways teas - ing you,
you hate to have me call you pret - ty ba - by;
I real - ly thought that I was pleas - ing you, for you're
just a ba - by to me. Your cun - ning lit - tle dim - ples and your
ba - by talk and ba - by walk and
ba - by stare, your
cur - ly hair; your ba - by smile makes life worth while, you're

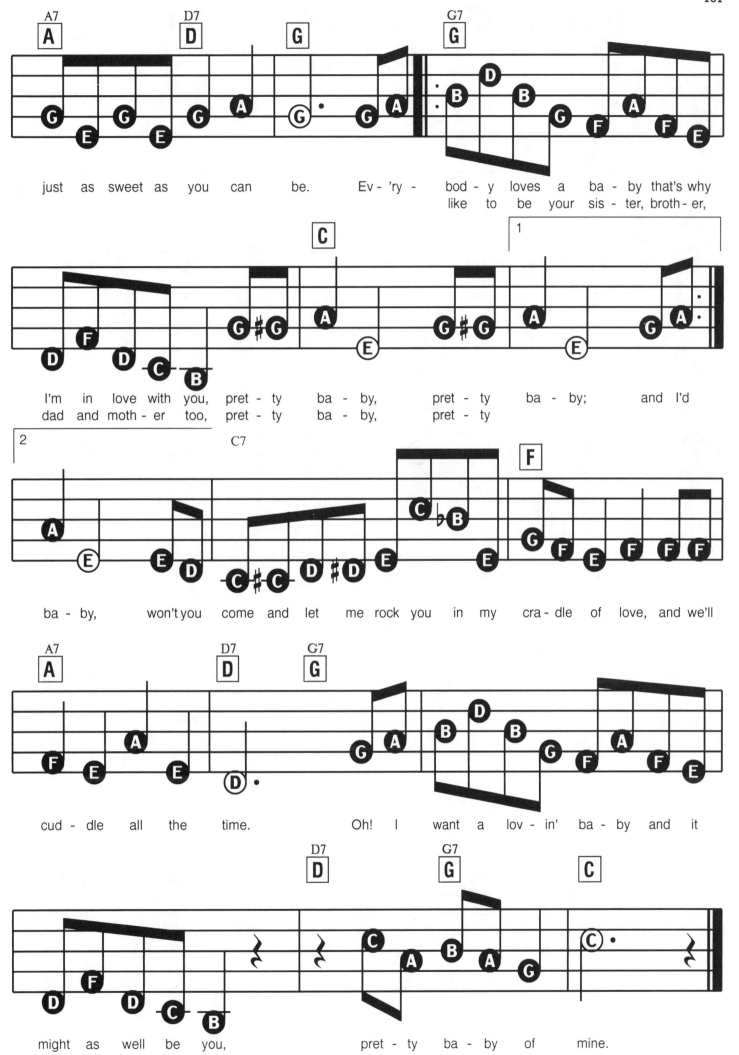

A Pretty Girl Is Like a Melody

from the 1919 Stage Production ZIEGFELD FOLLIES
from THE GREAT ZIEGFELD

Registration 8
Rhythm: Fox Trot or Ballad

Words and Music by
Irving Berlin

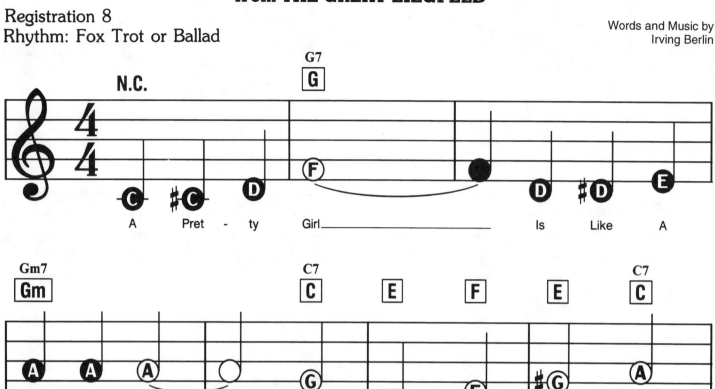

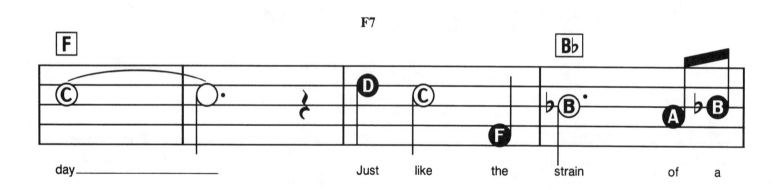

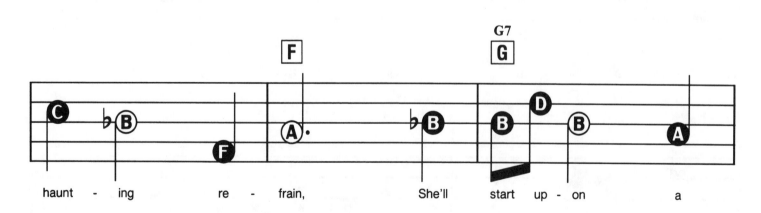

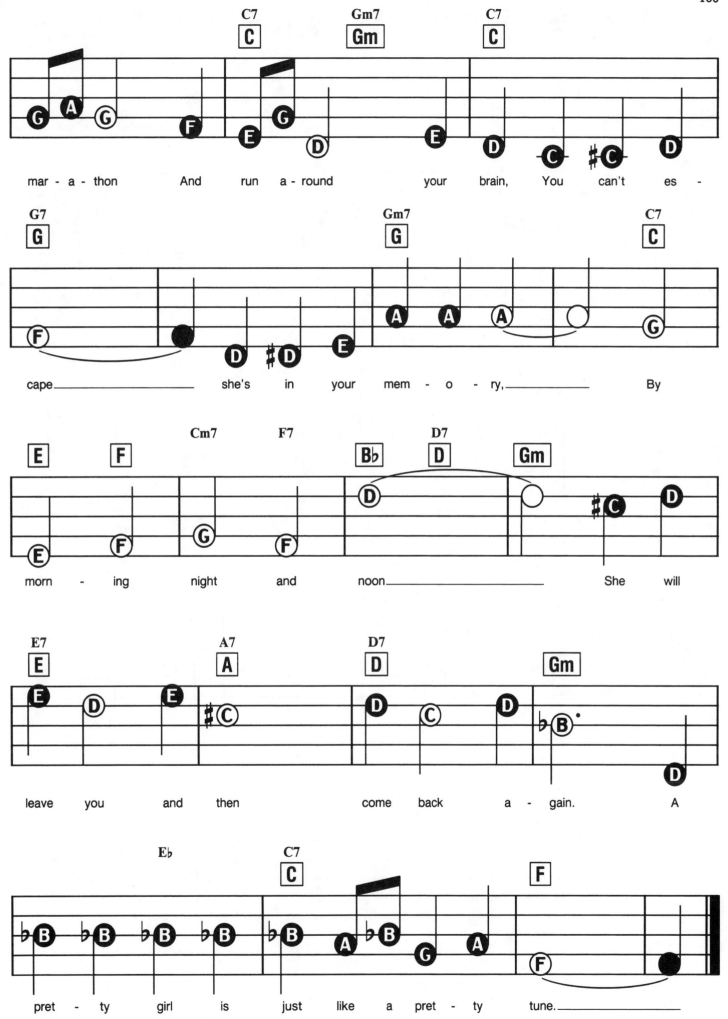

Put Your Arms Around Me, Honey

Registration 9
Rhythm: Fox Trot

Words by Junie McCree
Music by Albert von Tilzer

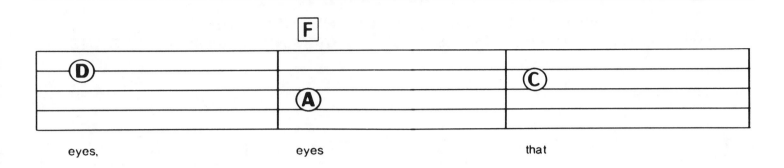

eyes,   eyes   that

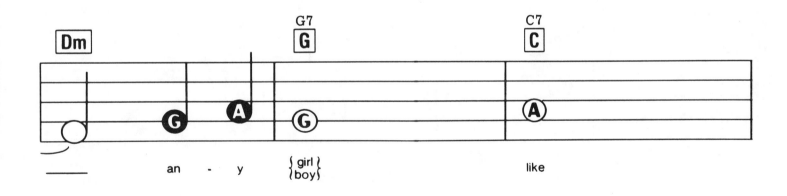

I just i - dol - ize.   I nev - er knew ___

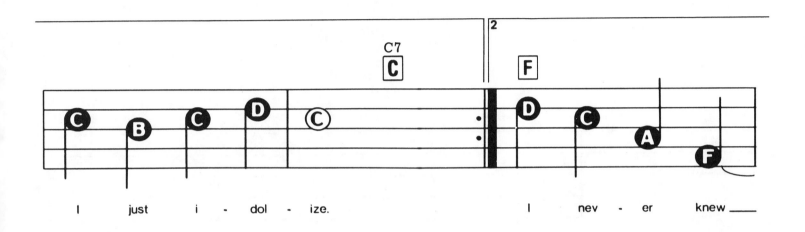

___ an - y {girl}{boy} like

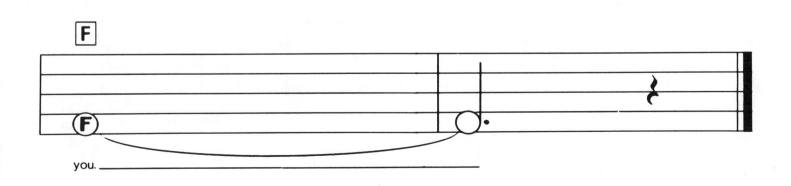

you. ___

Say It with Music

from the 1921 Stage Production MUSIC BOX REVUE
from the 20th Century Fox Motion Picture ALEXANDER'S RAGTIME BAND

Registration 2
Rhythm: Swing

Words and Music by
Irving Berlin

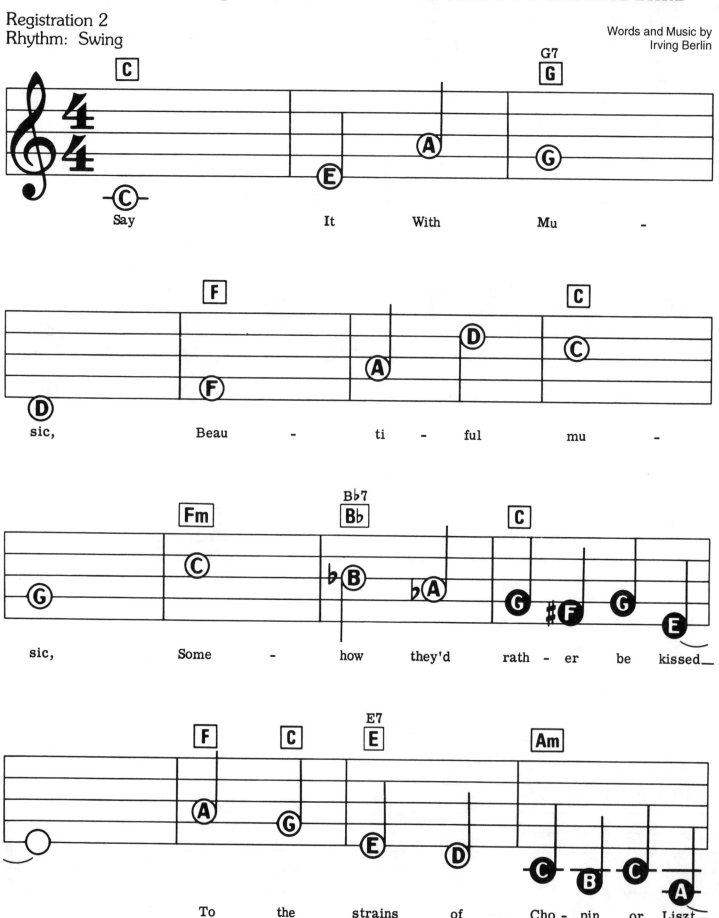

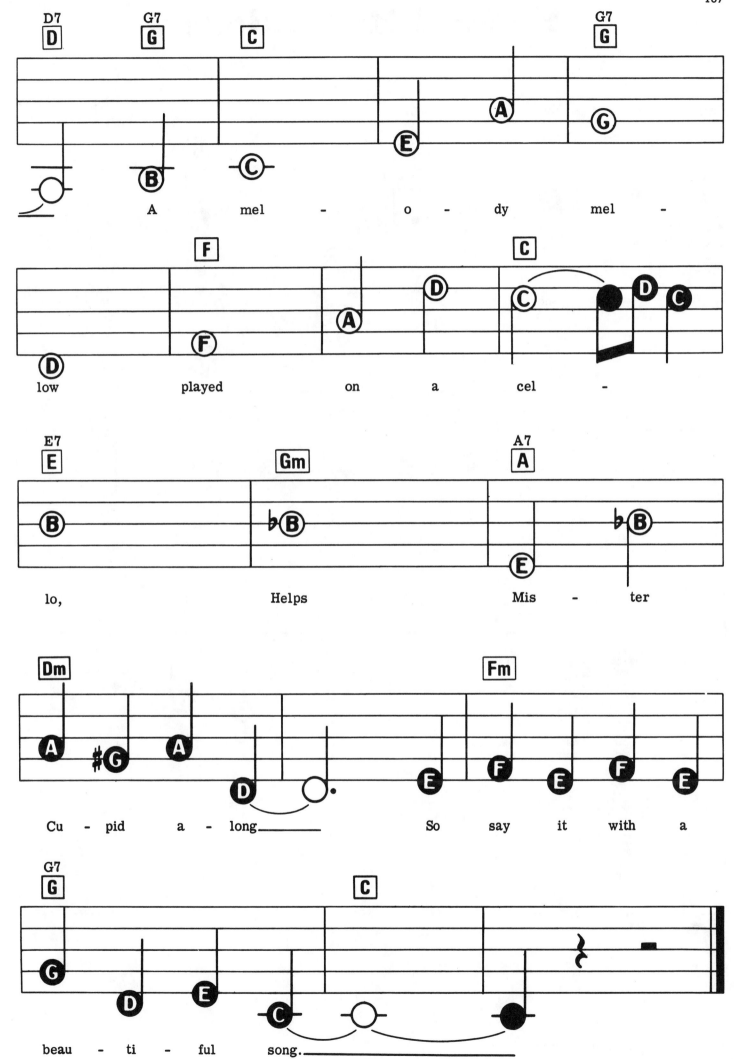

Second Hand Rose

Registration 8
Rhythm: Fox Trot or Swing

Words by Grant Clarke
Music by James F. Hanley

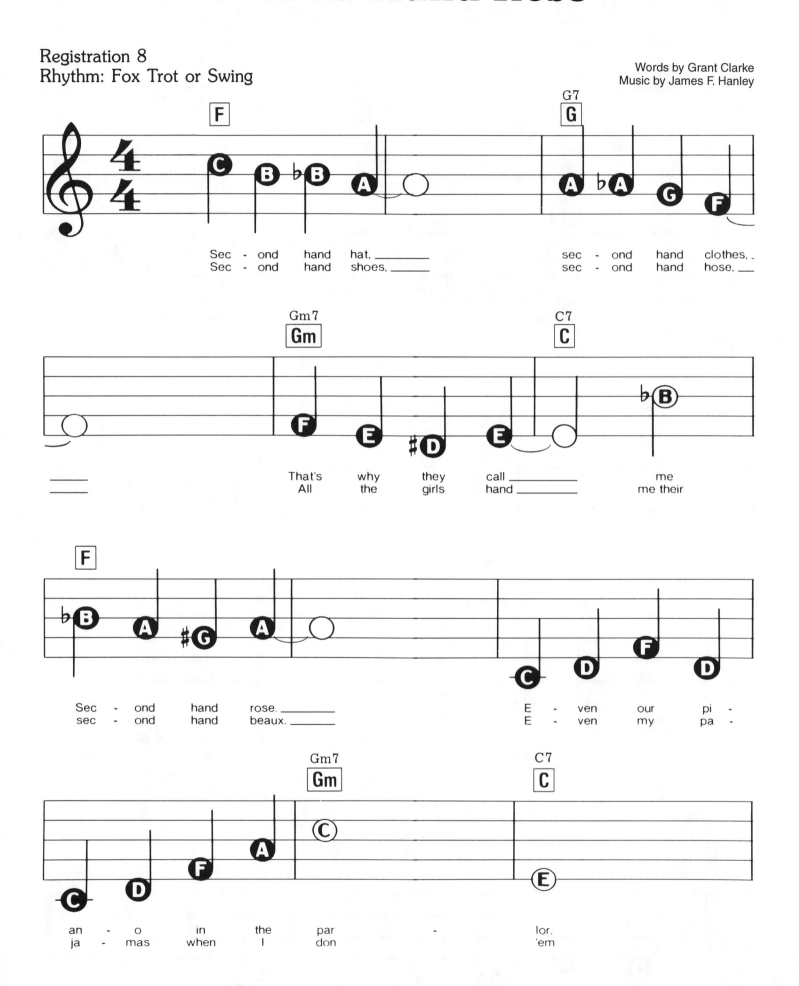

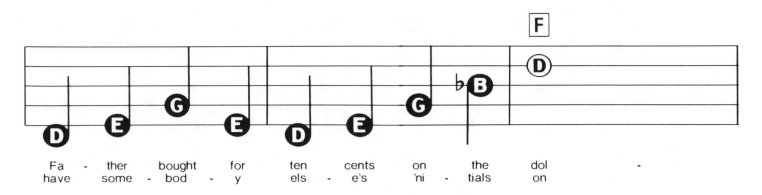

Fa - ther bought for ten cents on the dol -
have some - bod - y els - e's 'ni - tials on

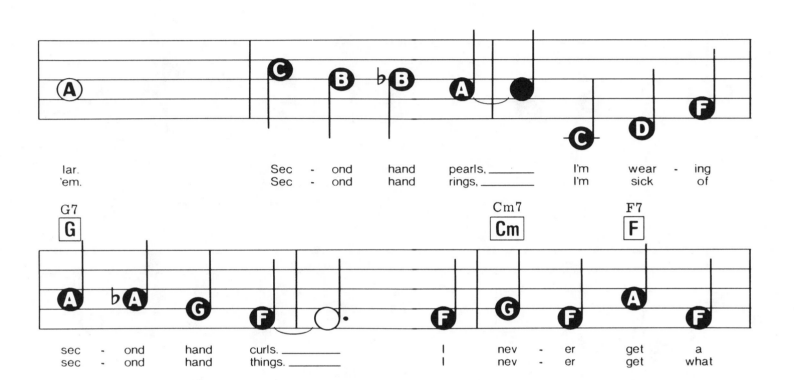

lar.   Sec - ond hand pearls, _____ I'm wear - ing
'em.   Sec - ond hand rings, _____ I'm sick of

sec - ond hand curls. _____ I nev - er get a
sec - ond hand things. _____ I nev - er get what

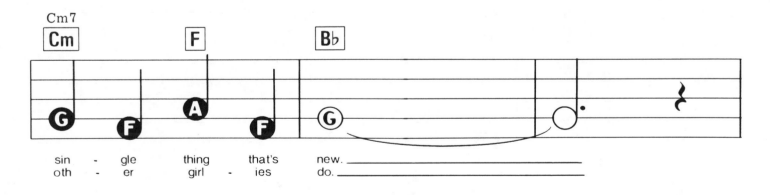

sin - gle thing that's new. _____
oth - er thing girl - ies do. _____

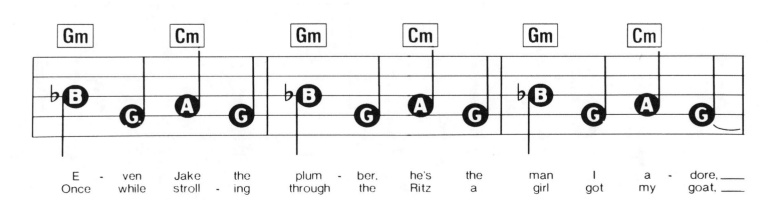

E - ven Jake the plum - ber. he's the man I a - dore, ___
Once while stroll - ing through the Ritz a girl got my goat, ___

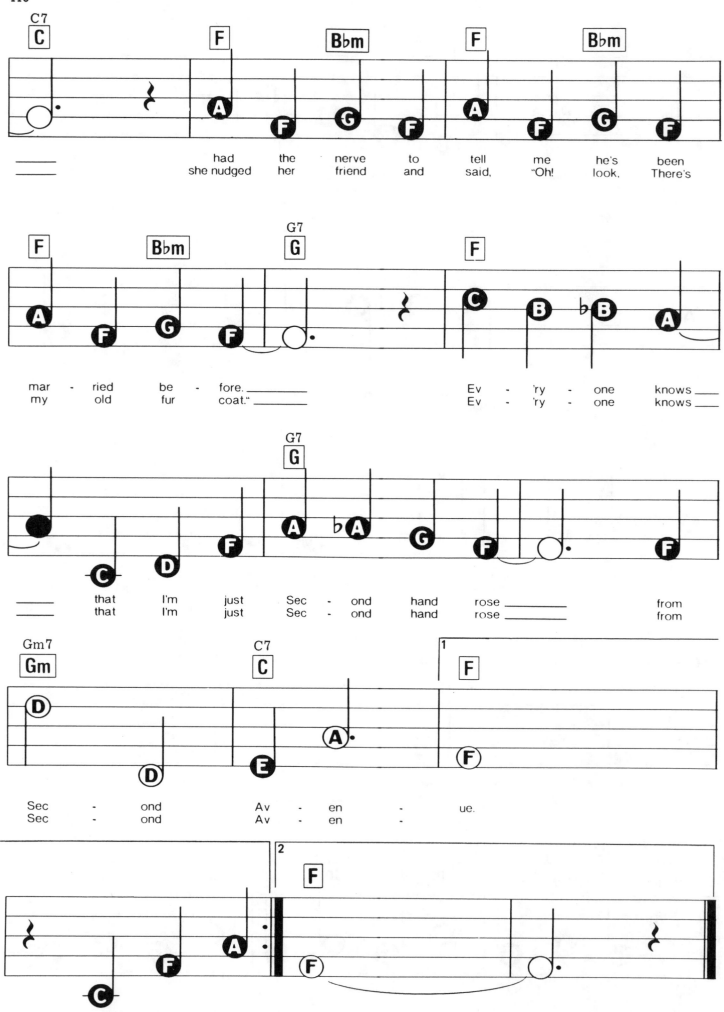

Stumbling

Registration 8
Rhythm: Shuffle or Swing

Words and Music by
Zez Confrey

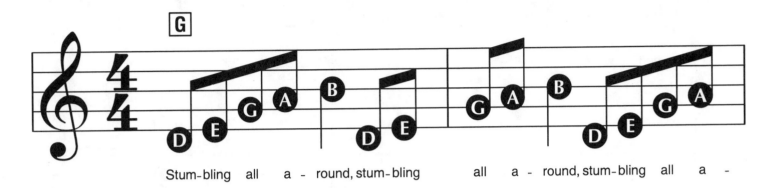

Stum-bling all a - round, stum-bling all a - round, stum-bling all a -

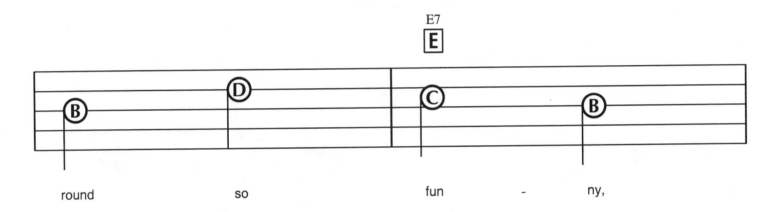

round so fun - ny,

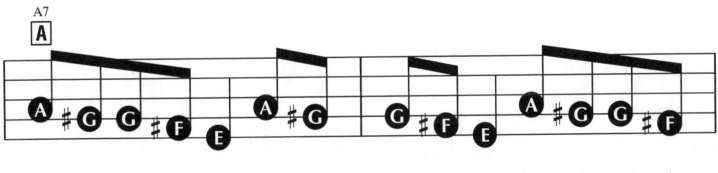

stum - bling here and there, stum-bling ev - 'ry - where and I must de -

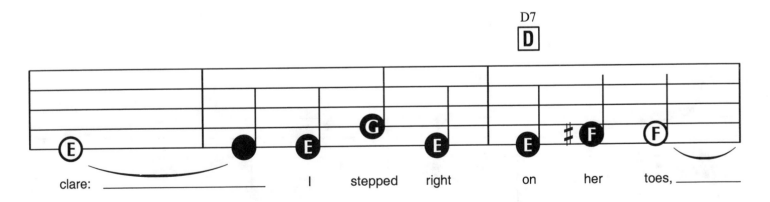

clare: _____ I stepped right on her toes, _____

112

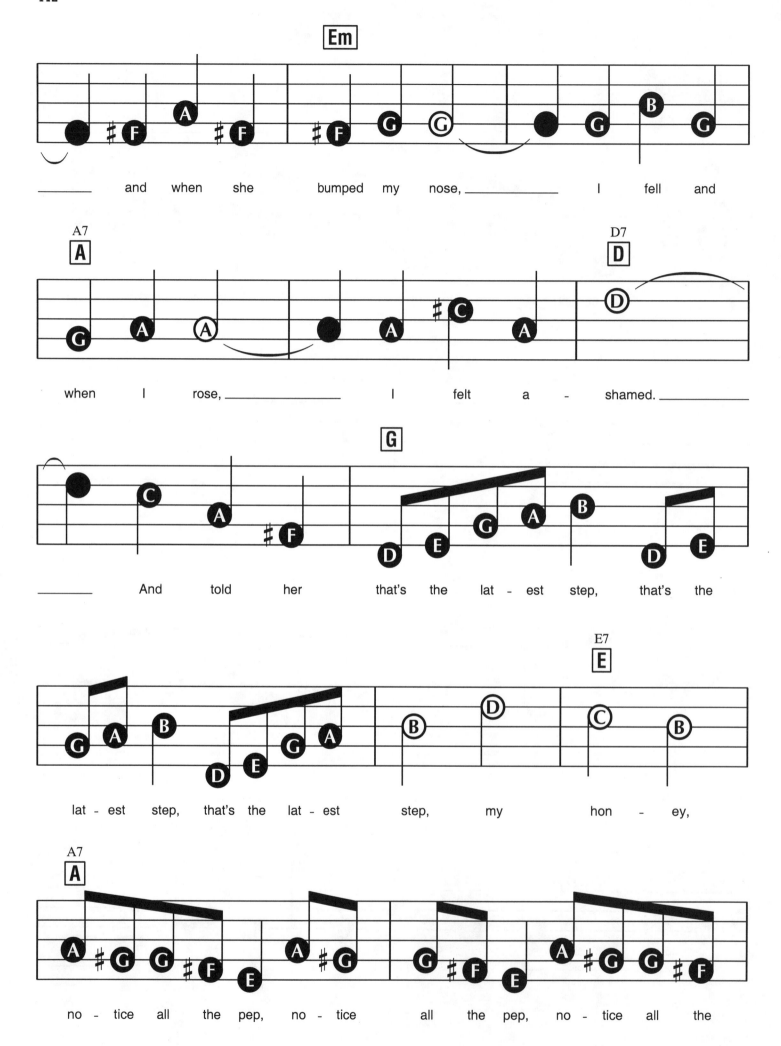

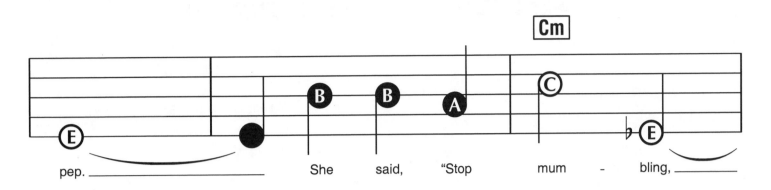

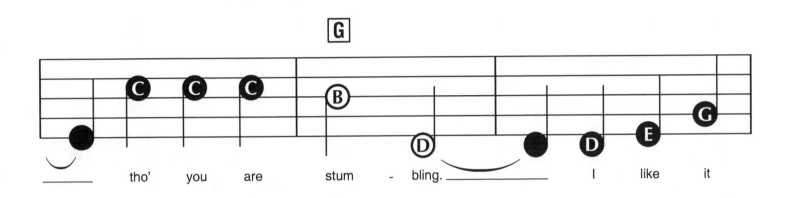

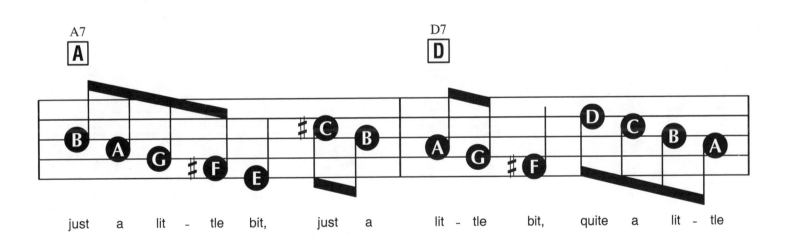

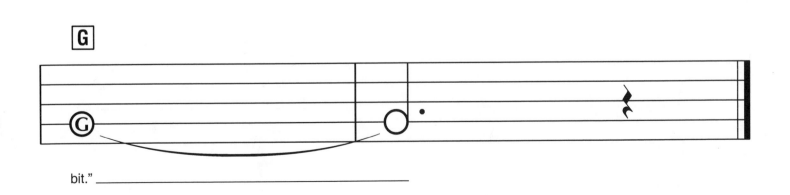

The Sheik of Araby

Registration 9
Rhythm: Swing or Jazz

Words by Harry B. Smith and Francis Wheeler
Music by Ted Snyder

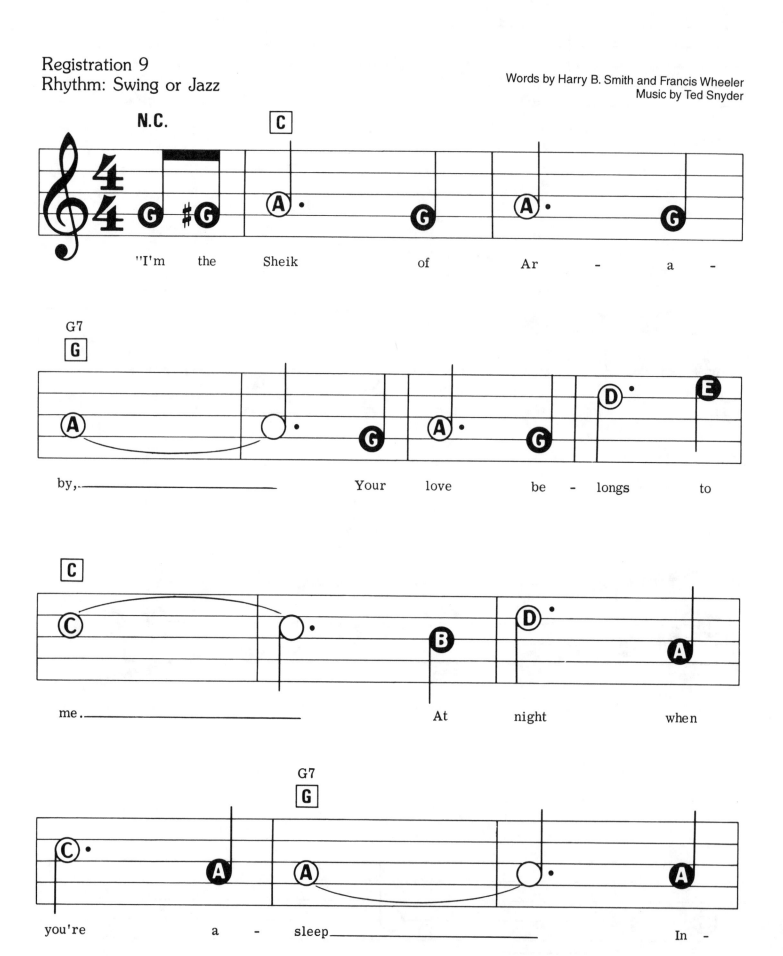

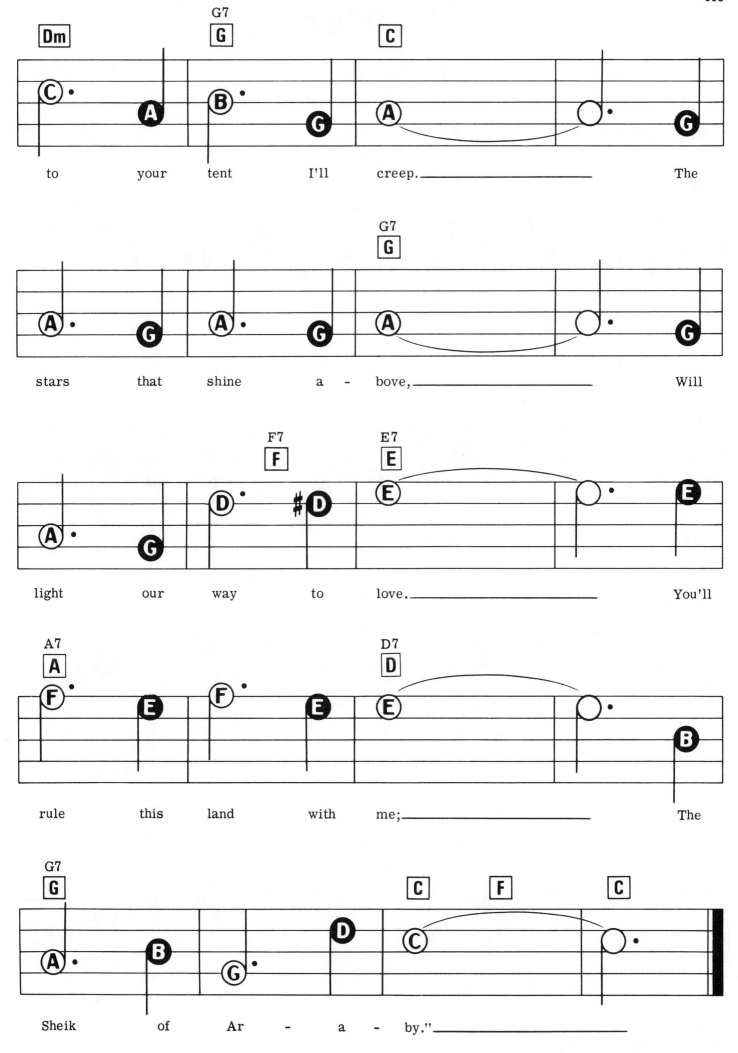

Smiles

Registration 5
Rhythm: Fox Trot or Swing

Words by J. Will Callahan
Music by Lee S. Roberts

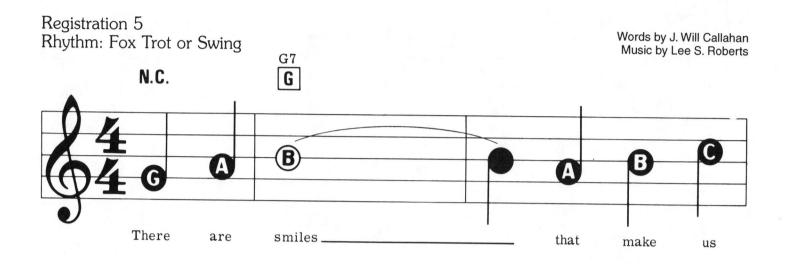

There are smiles _____ that make us

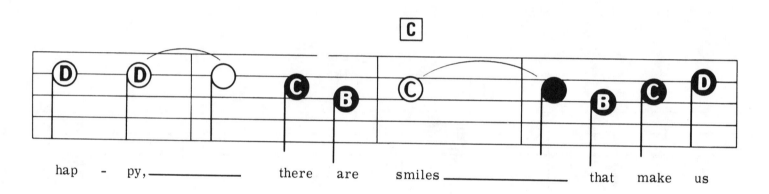

hap - py, _____ there are smiles _____ that make us

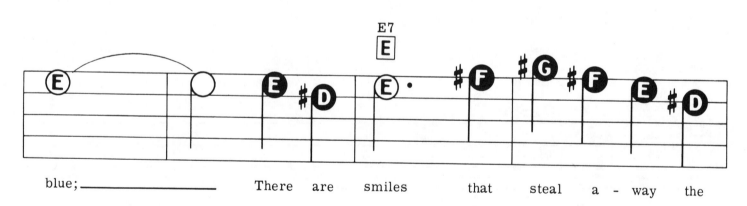

blue; _____ There are smiles that steal a - way the

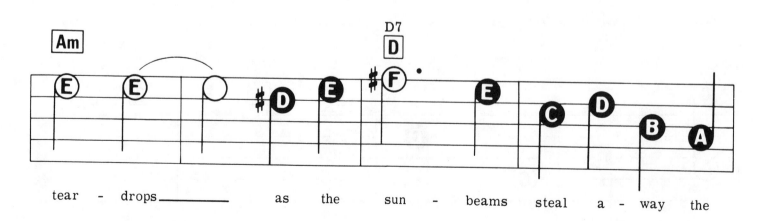

tear - drops _____ as the sun - beams steal a - way the

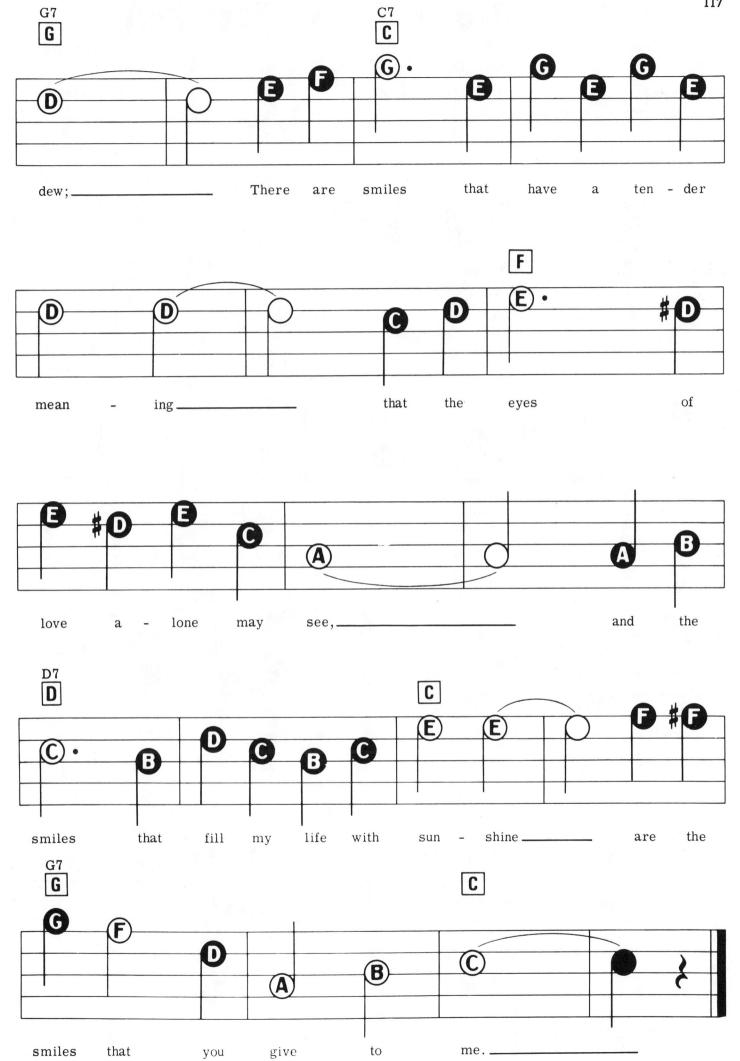

Somebody Stole My Gal

Registration 2
Rhythm: Fox Trot or Swing

Words and Music by
Leo Wood

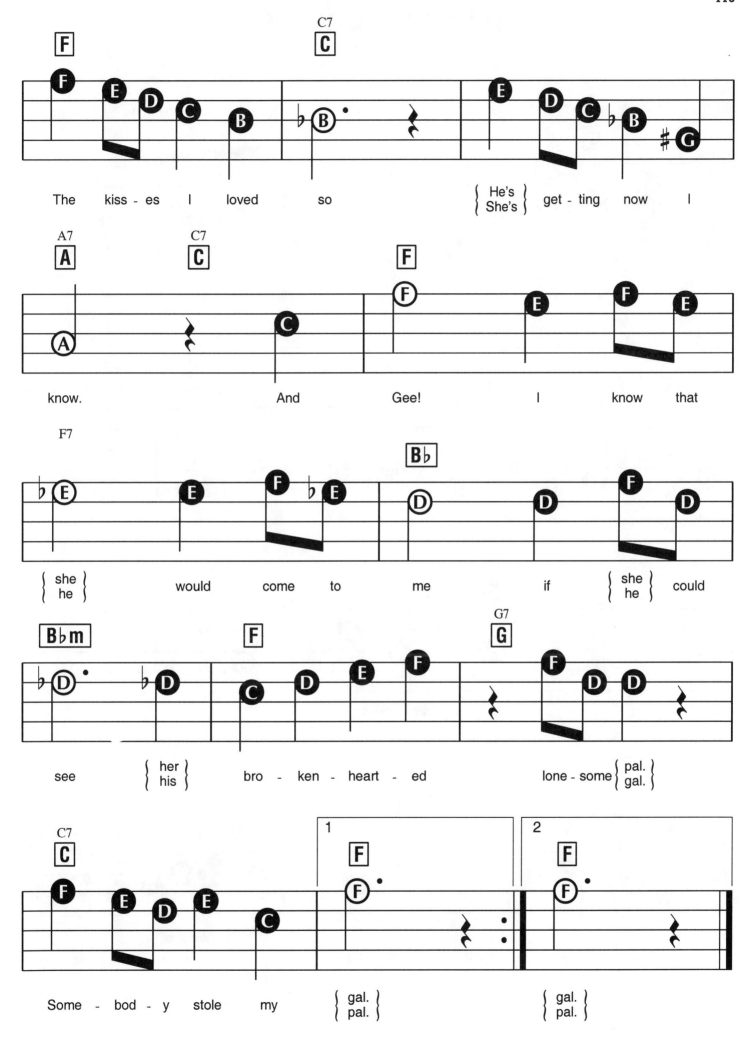

Sugar Blues

Registration 3
Rhythm: Swing or Fox Trot

Words by Lucy Fletcher
Music by Clarence Williams

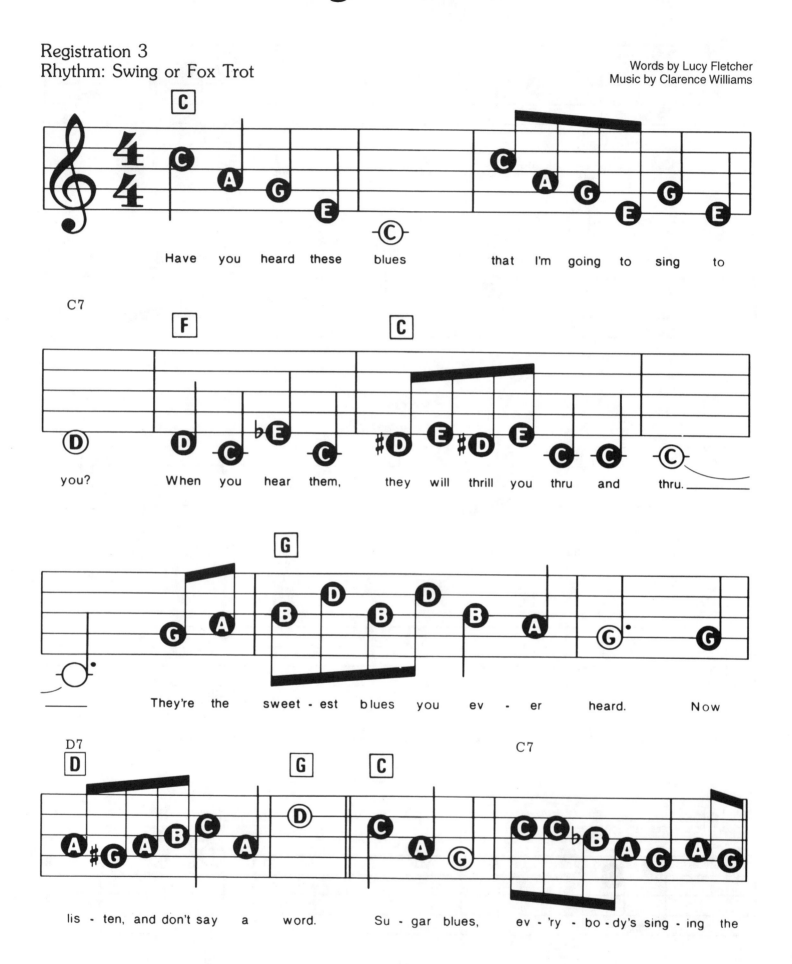

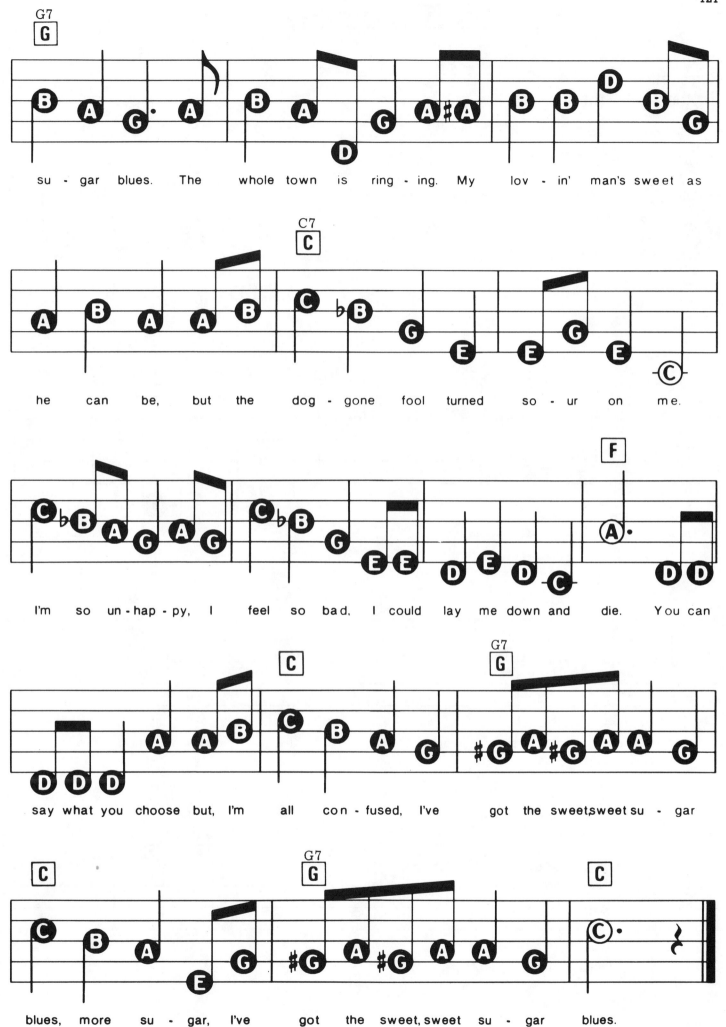

Swanee

Registration 9
Rhythm: Fox Trot or Swing

Words by Irving Caesar
Music by George Gershwin

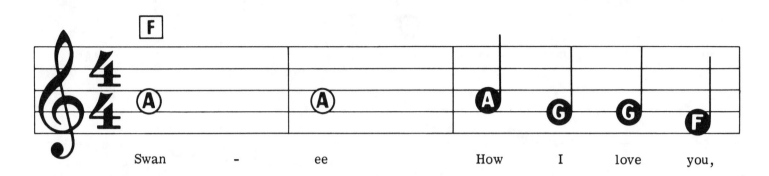

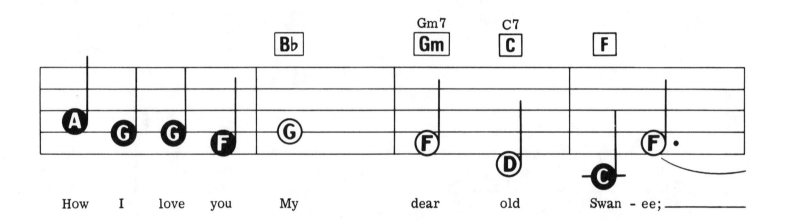

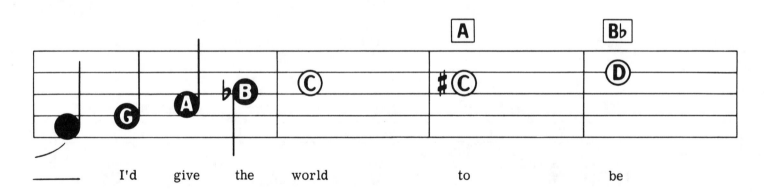

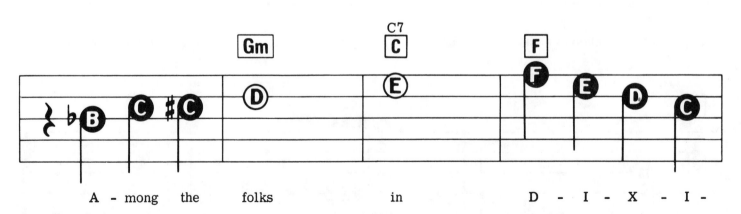

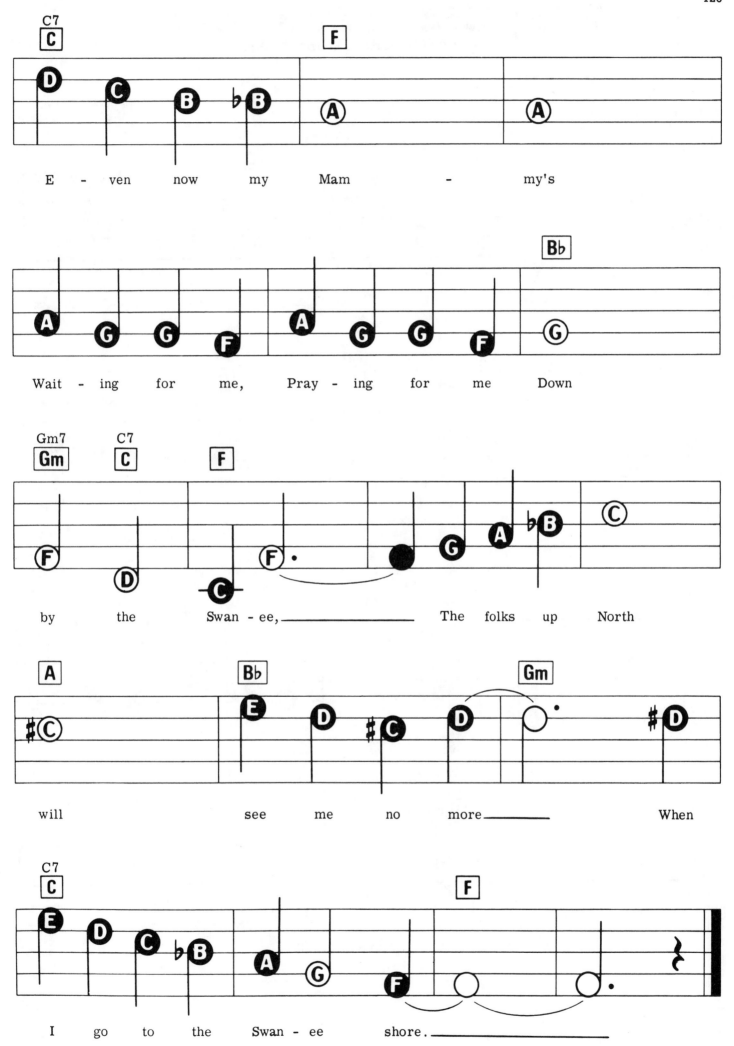

They Didn't Believe Me

from THE GIRL FROM UTAH

Registration 2
Rhythm: Ballad or Swing

Words by Herbert Reynolds
Music by Jerome Kern

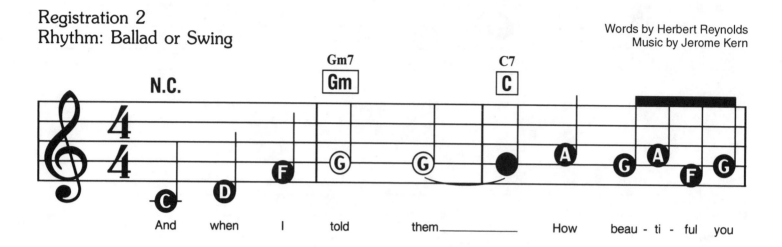

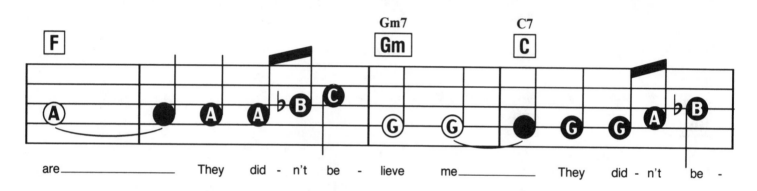

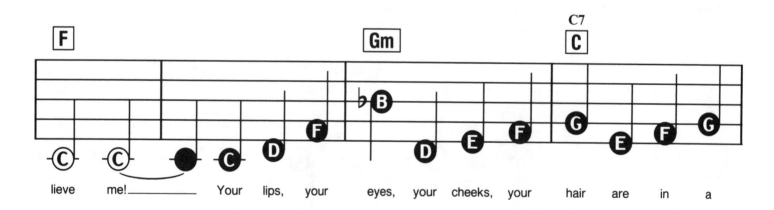

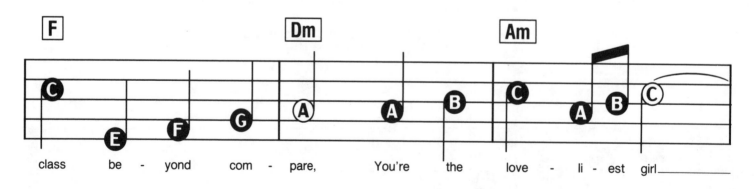

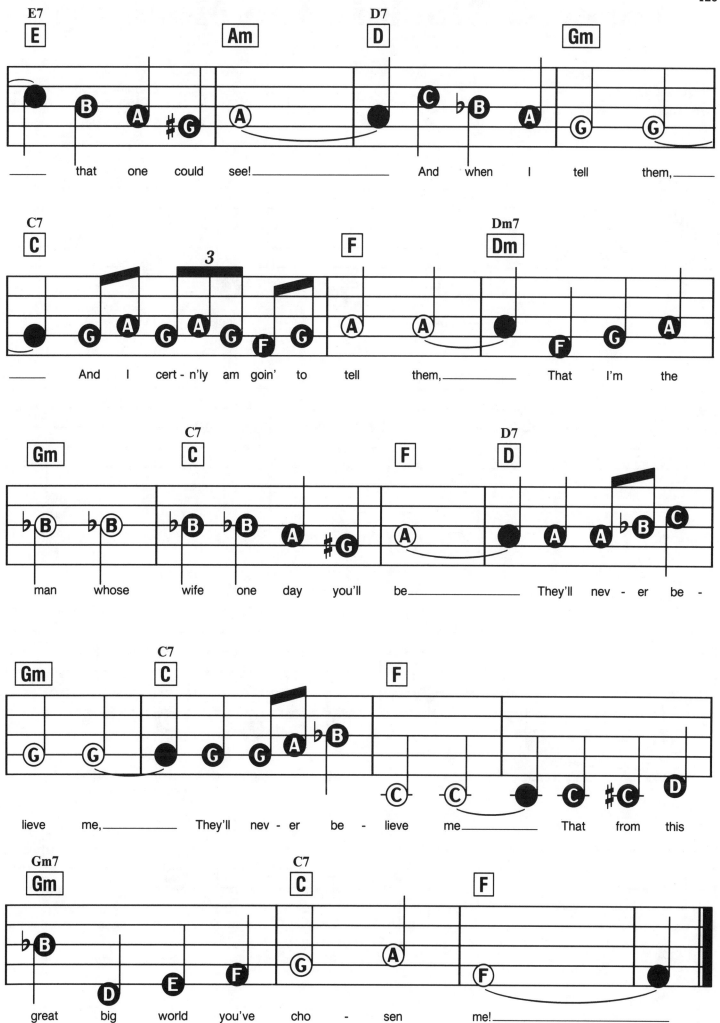

Three O'Clock in the Morning

Registration 10
Rhythm: Waltz

Words by Dorothy Terriss
Music by Julian Robledo

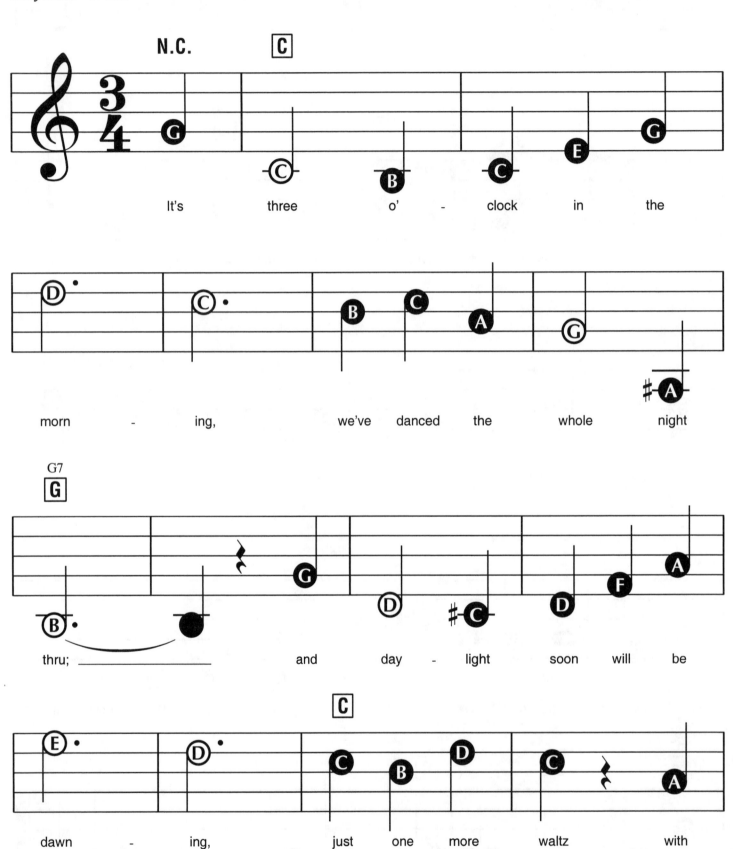

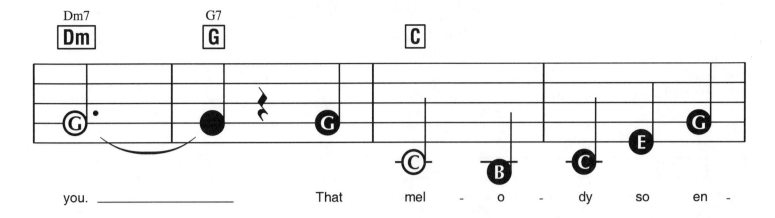

you. _____ That mel - o - dy so en -

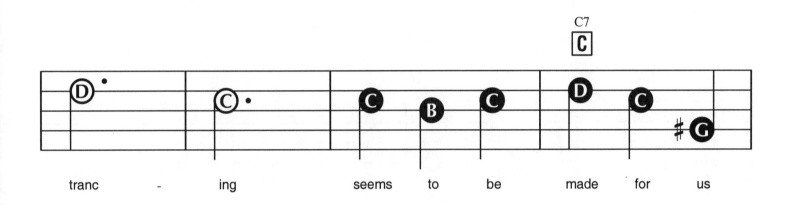

tranc - ing seems to be made for us

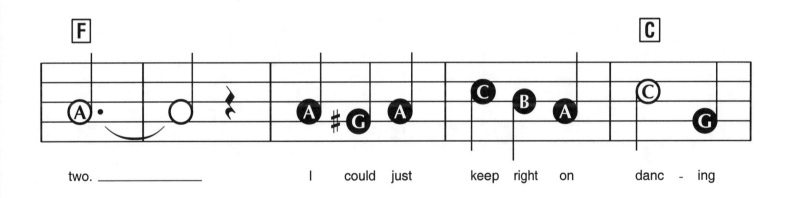

two. _____ I could just keep right on danc - ing

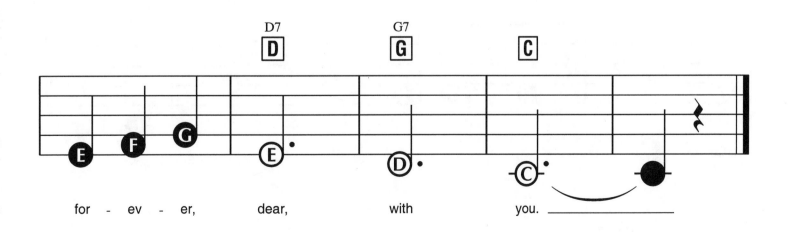

for - ev - er, dear, with you. _____

Tiger Rag
(Hold That Tiger)

Registration 4
Rhythm: Swing or Ragtime

Words by Harry DeCosta
Music by Original Dixieland Jazz Band

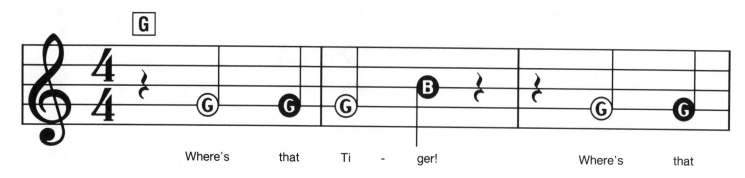

Where's that Ti - ger! Where's that

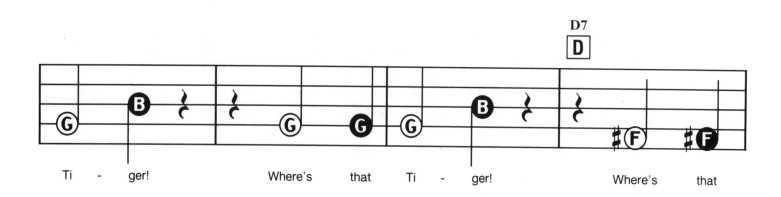

Ti - ger! Where's that Ti - ger! Where's that

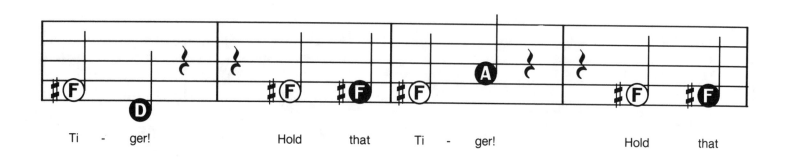

Ti - ger! Hold that Ti - ger! Hold that

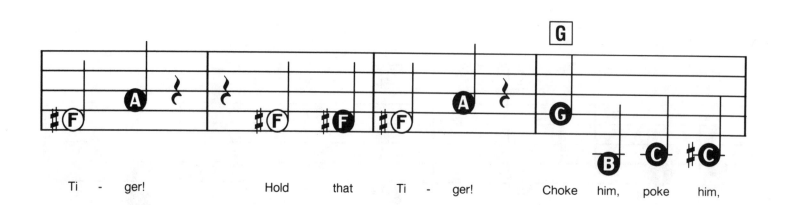

Ti - ger! Hold that Ti - ger! Choke him, poke him,

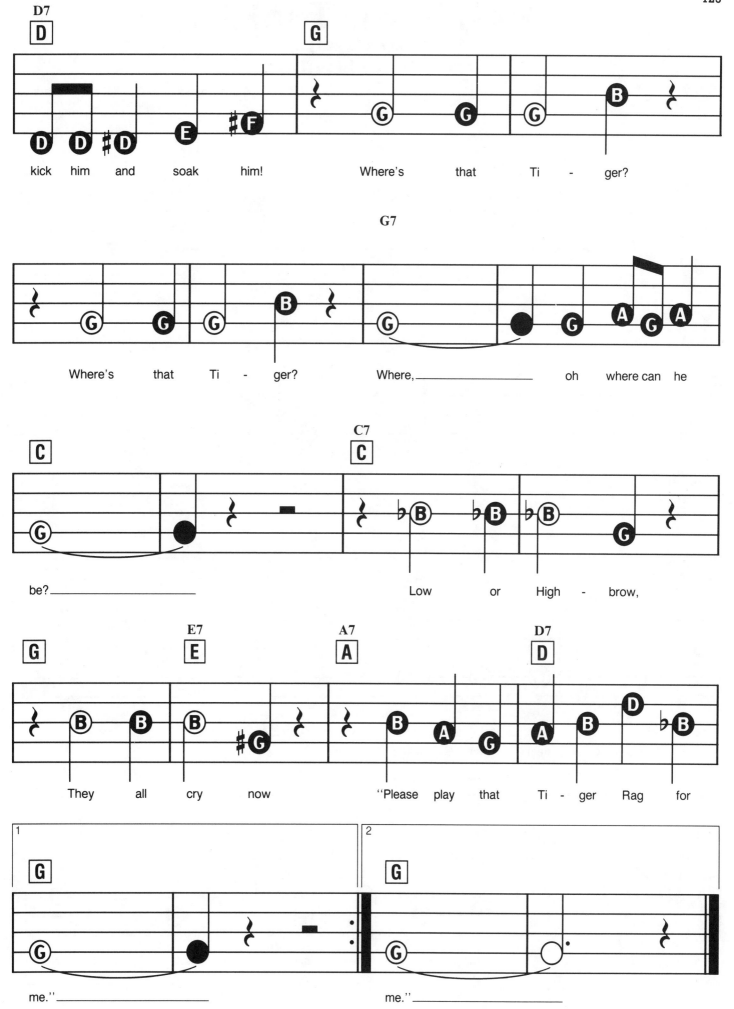

Toot, Toot, Tootsie!
(Good-bye!)
from THE JAZZ SINGER

Registration 4
Rhythm: Swing

Words and Music by Gus Kahn, Ernie Erdman,
Dan Russo and Ted Fiorito

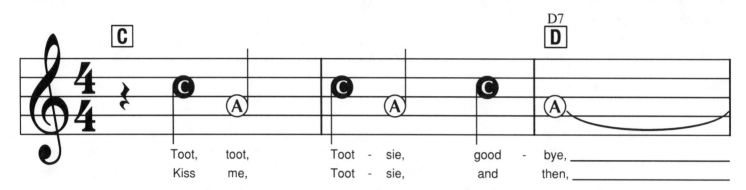

Toot, toot, Toot - sie, good - bye, ___
Kiss me, Toot - sie, and then, ___

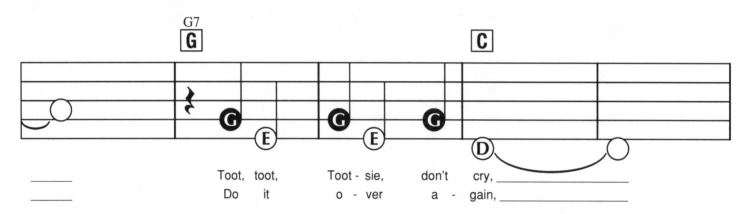

___ Toot, toot, Toot - sie, don't cry, ___
___ Do it o - ver a - gain, ___

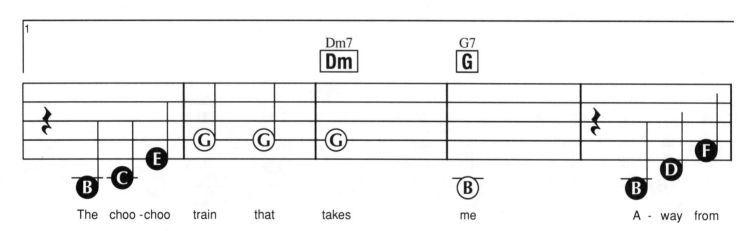

The choo -choo train that takes me A - way from

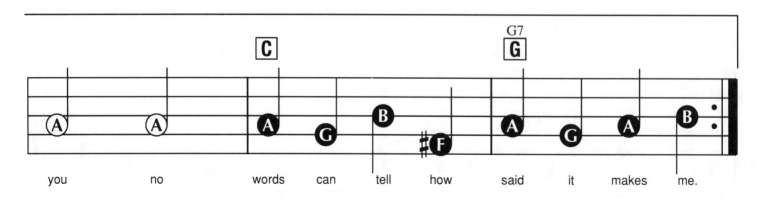

you no words can tell how said it makes me.

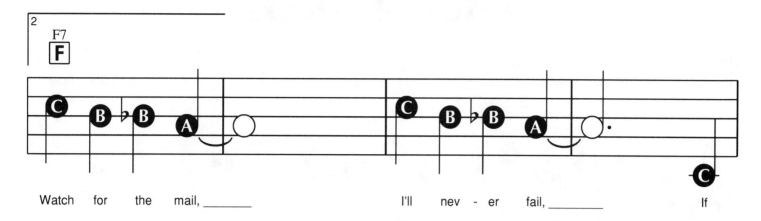

Watch for the mail, _____ I'll nev - er fail, _____ If

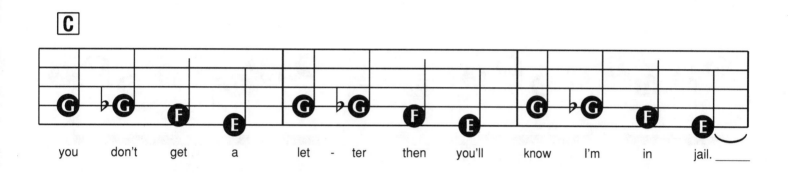

you don't get a let - ter then you'll know I'm in jail. _____

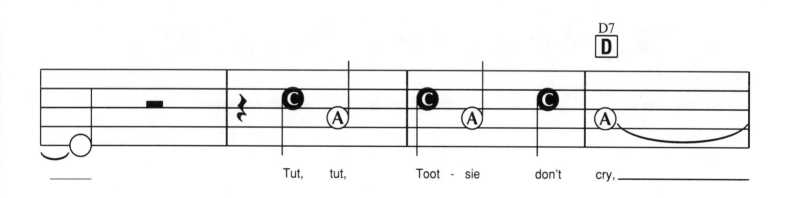

_____ Tut, tut, Toot - sie don't cry, _____

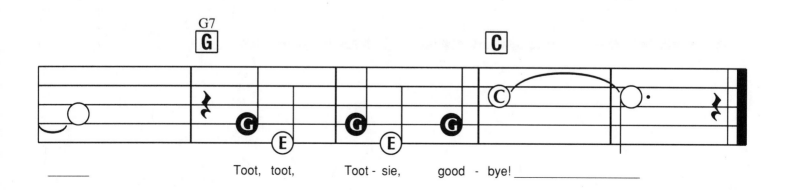

_____ Toot, toot, Toot - sie, good - bye! _____

Twelfth Street Rag

Registration 5
Rhythm: Shuffle or Swing

By Euday L. Bowman

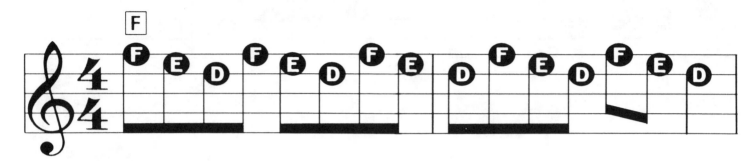

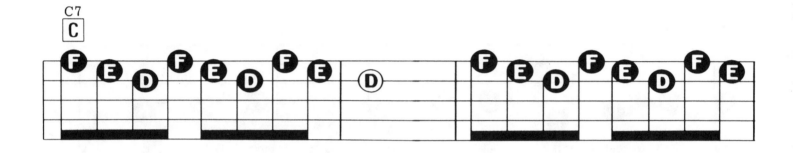

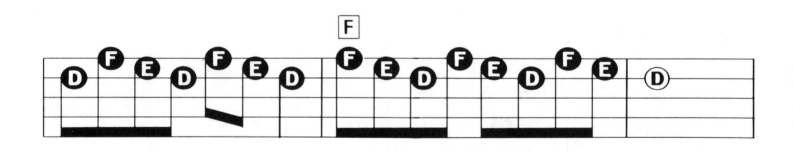

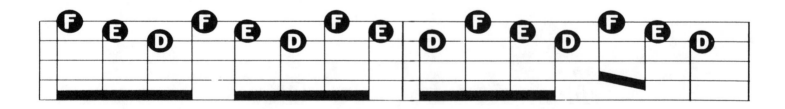

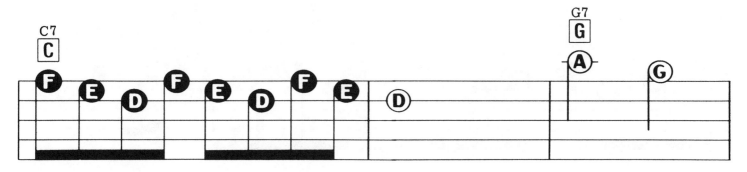

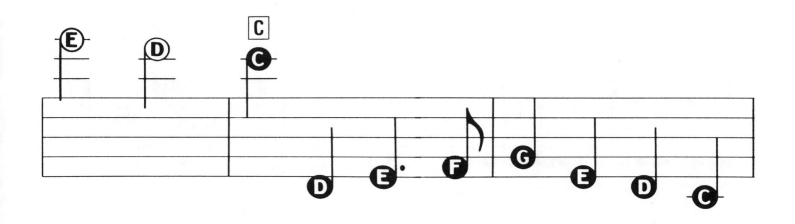

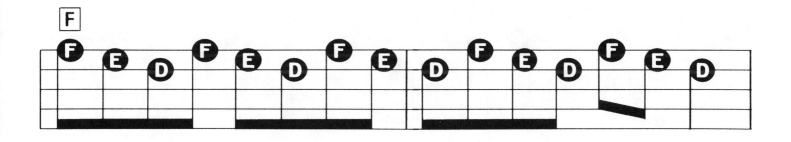

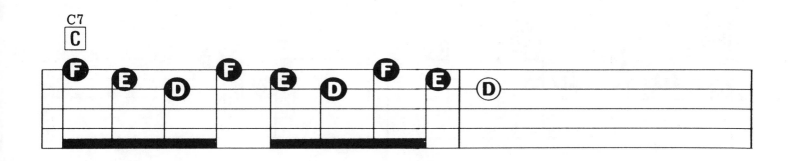

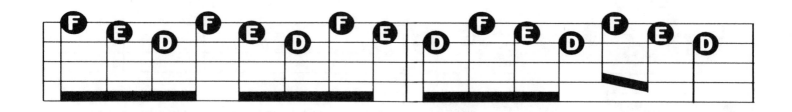

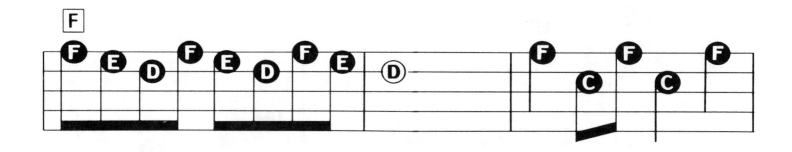

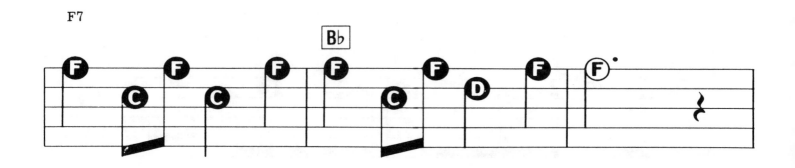

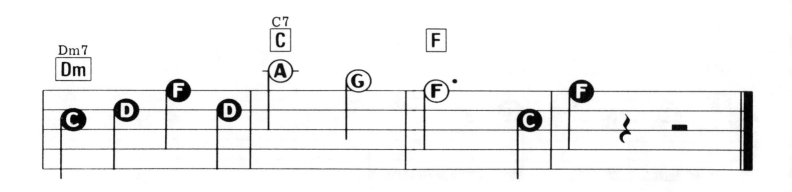

The Wang Wang Blues

Registration 8
Rhythm: Swing

Words and Music by Leo Wood, Gus Mueller,
Buster Johnson and Henry Busse

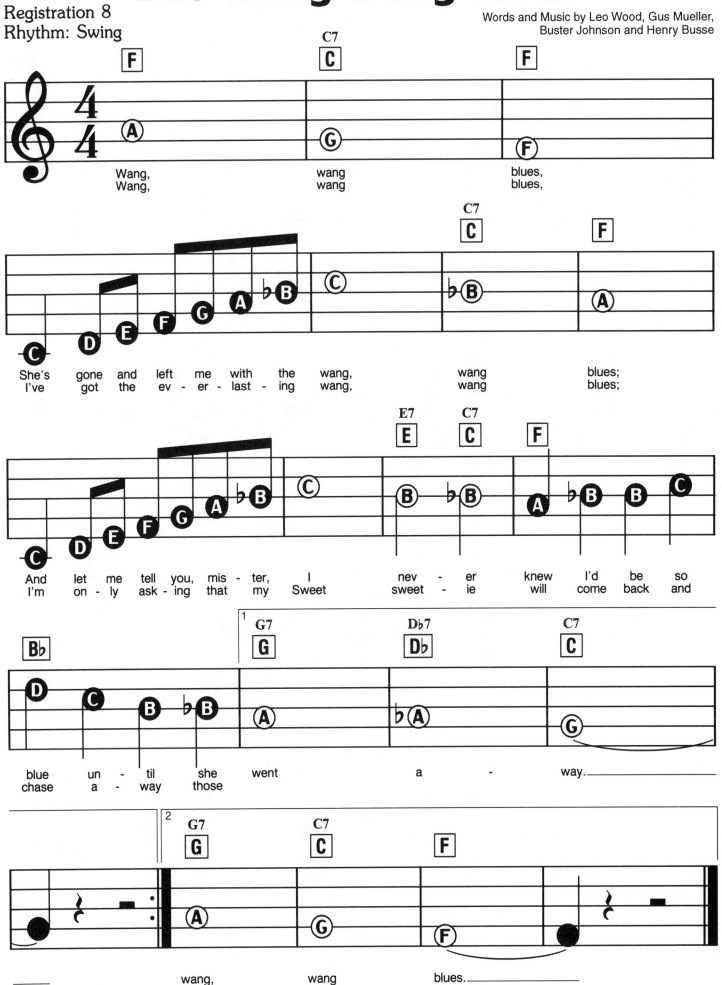

Waiting for the Robert E. Lee

Registration 3
Rhythm: Fox Trot or Jazz

Words by L. Wolfe Gilbert
Music by Lewis F. Muir

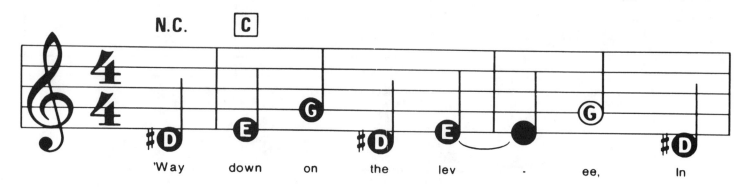

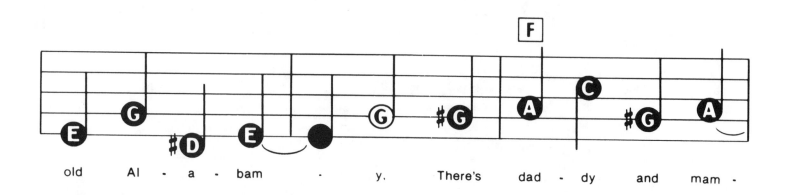

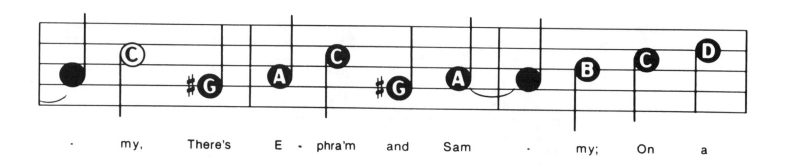

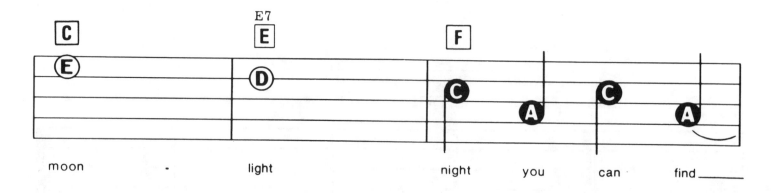

137

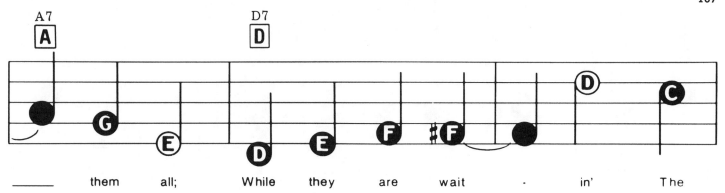

them all; While they are wait - in' The

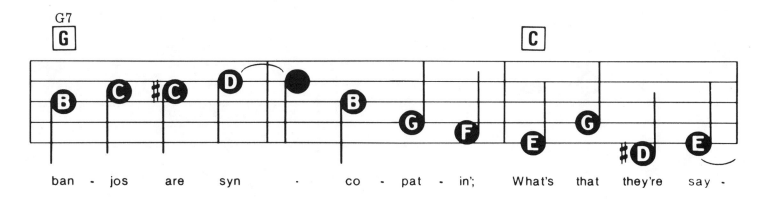

ban - jos are syn - co - pat - in'; What's that they're say -

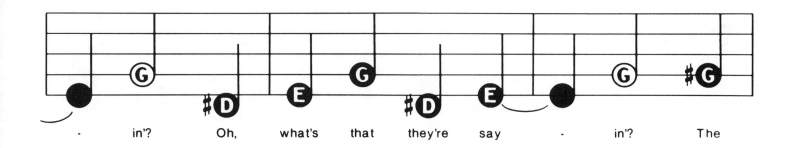

- in'? Oh, what's that they're say - in'? The

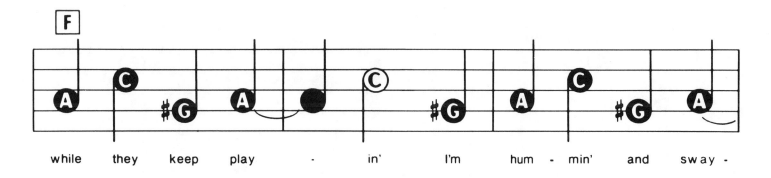

while they keep play - in' I'm hum - min' and sway -

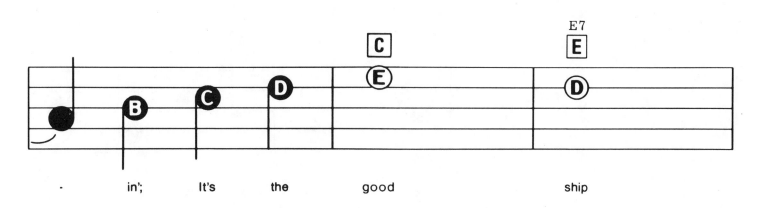

- in'; It's the good ship

138

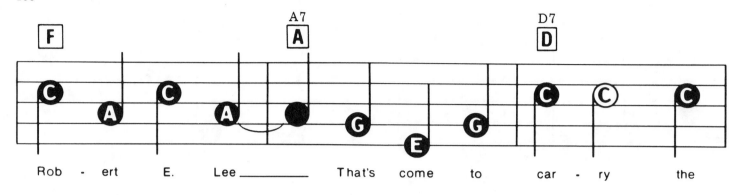

Rob - ert E. Lee _____ That's come to car - ry the

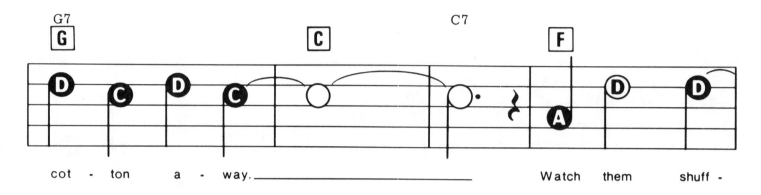

cot - ton a - way. _____ Watch them shuff -

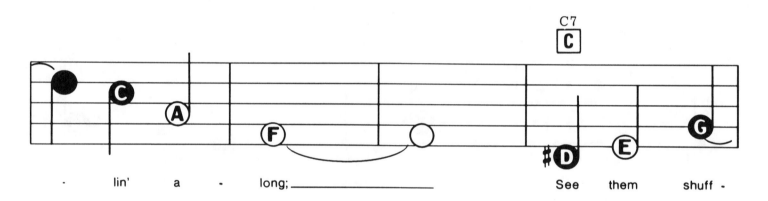

- lin' a - long; _____ See them shuff -

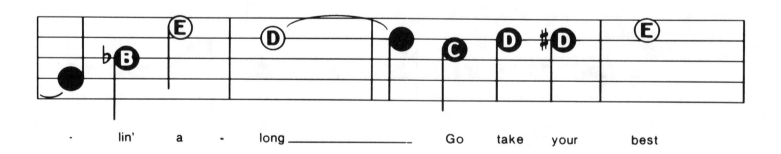

- lin' a - long _____ Go take your best

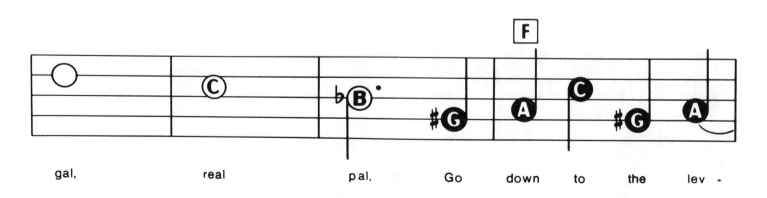

gal, real pal, Go down to the lev -

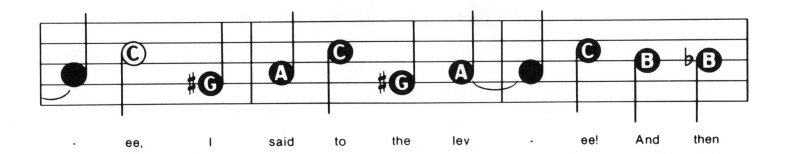

- ee, I said to the lev - ee! And then

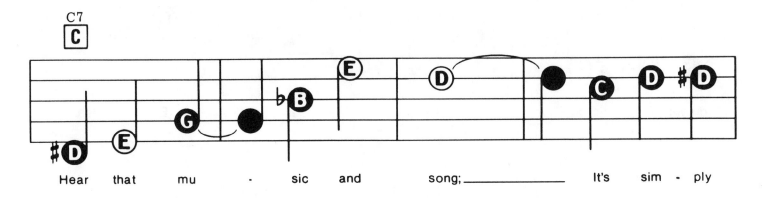

join that shuff - - lin' throng;_____

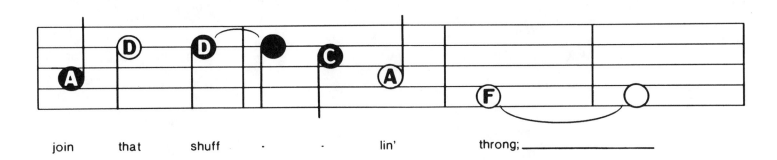

Hear that mu - sic and song;_____ It's sim - ply

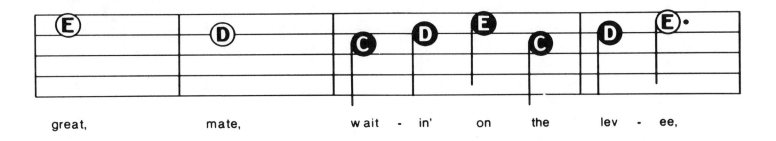

great, mate, wait - in' on the lev - ee,

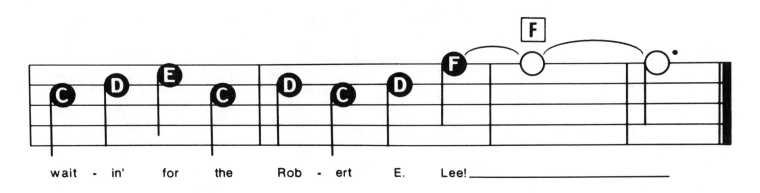

wait - in' for the Rob - ert E. Lee!_____

'Way Down Yonder
in New Orleans

Registration 7
Rhythm: Swing

*Words and Music by Henry Creamer
and J. Turner Layton*

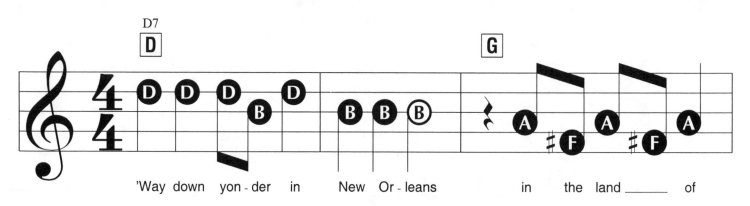

'Way down yon-der in New Or-leans in the land _____ of

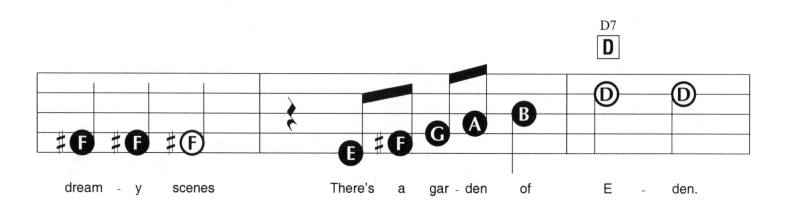

dream - y scenes There's a gar-den of E - den.

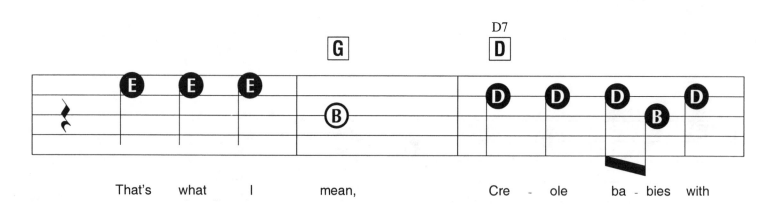

That's what I mean, Cre - ole ba - bies with

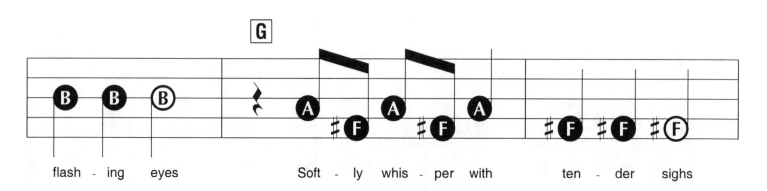

flash - ing eyes Soft - ly whis - per with ten - der sighs

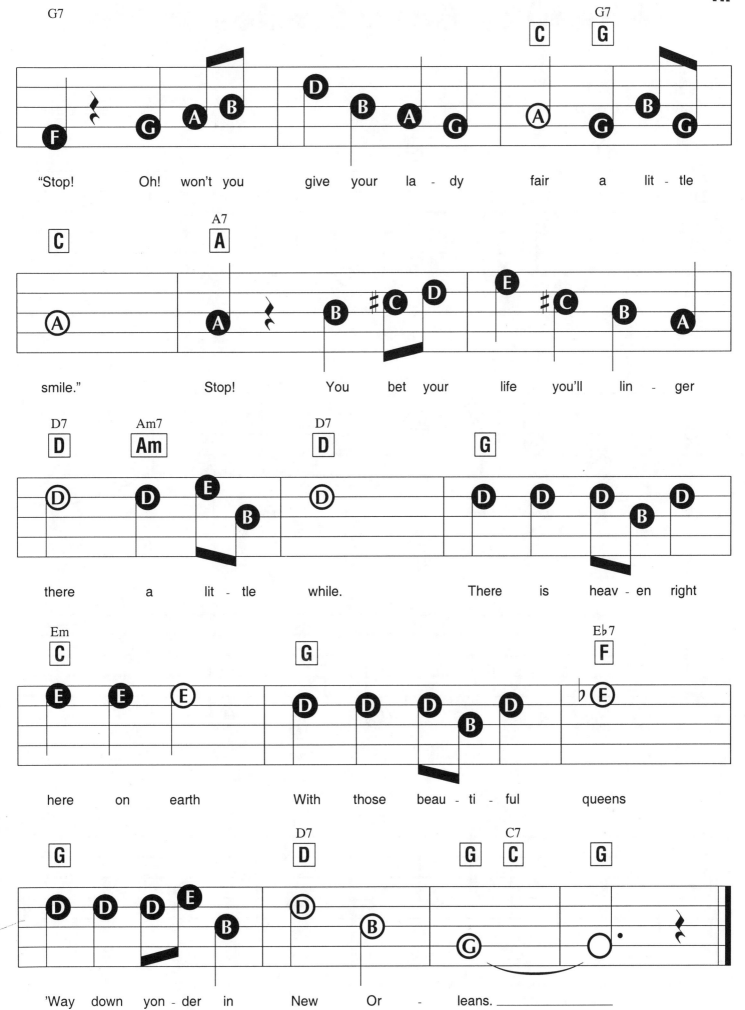

When My Baby Smiles at Me

Registration 1
Rhythm: Fox Trot or Swing

Words and Music by Harry von Tilzer, Andrew B. Sterling,
Bill Munro and Ted Lewis

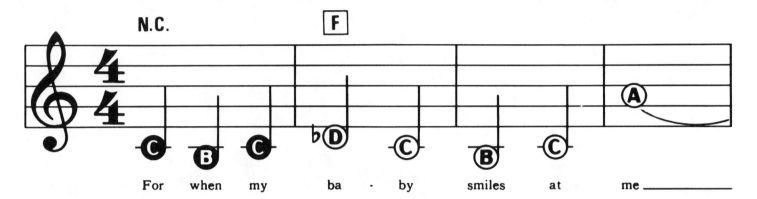

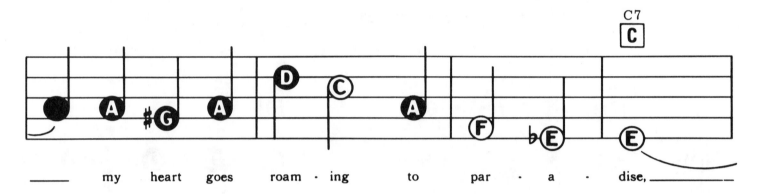

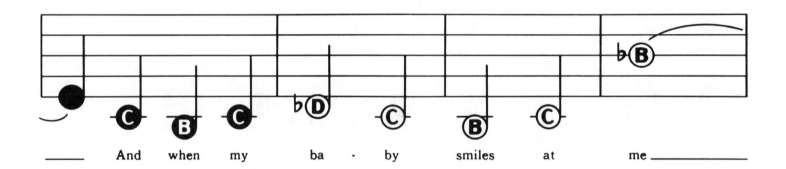

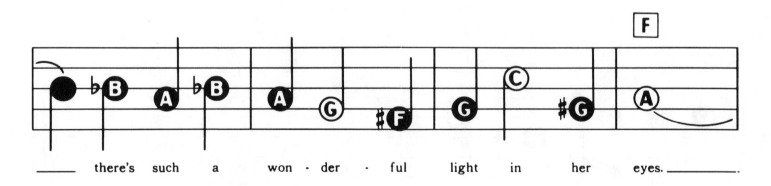

143

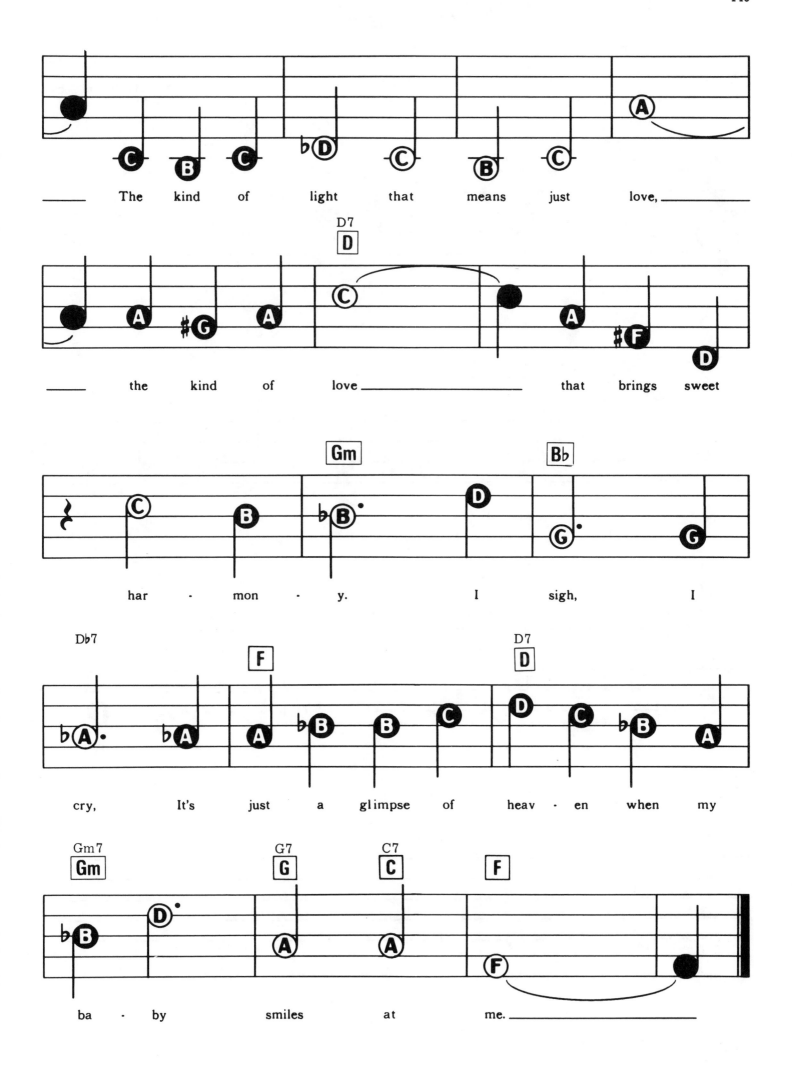

Whispering

Registration 4
Rhythm: Fox Trot or Swing

Words and Music by Richard Coburn,
John Schonberger and Vincent Rose

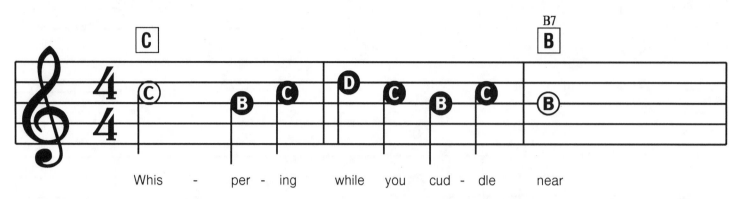

Whis - per - ing while you cud - dle near

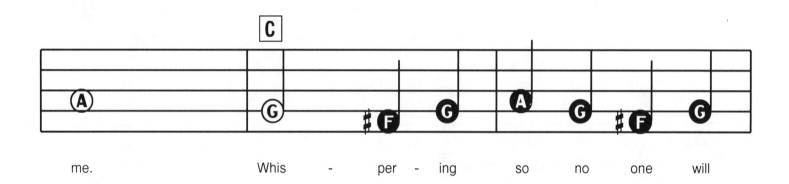

me.   Whis - per - ing so no one will

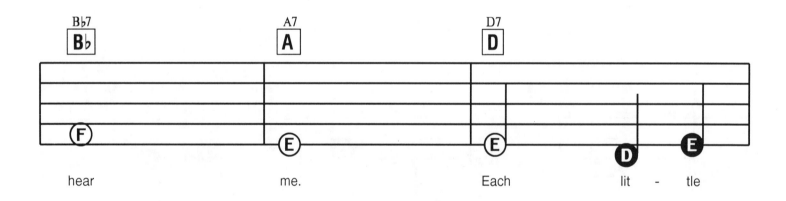

hear   me.   Each   lit - tle

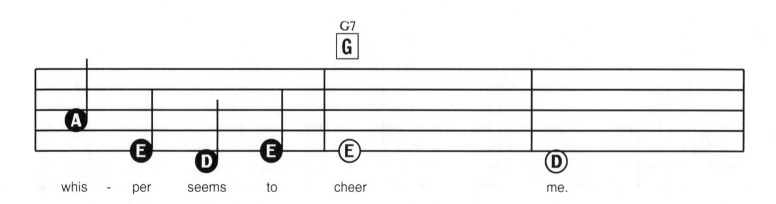

whis - per seems to cheer   me.

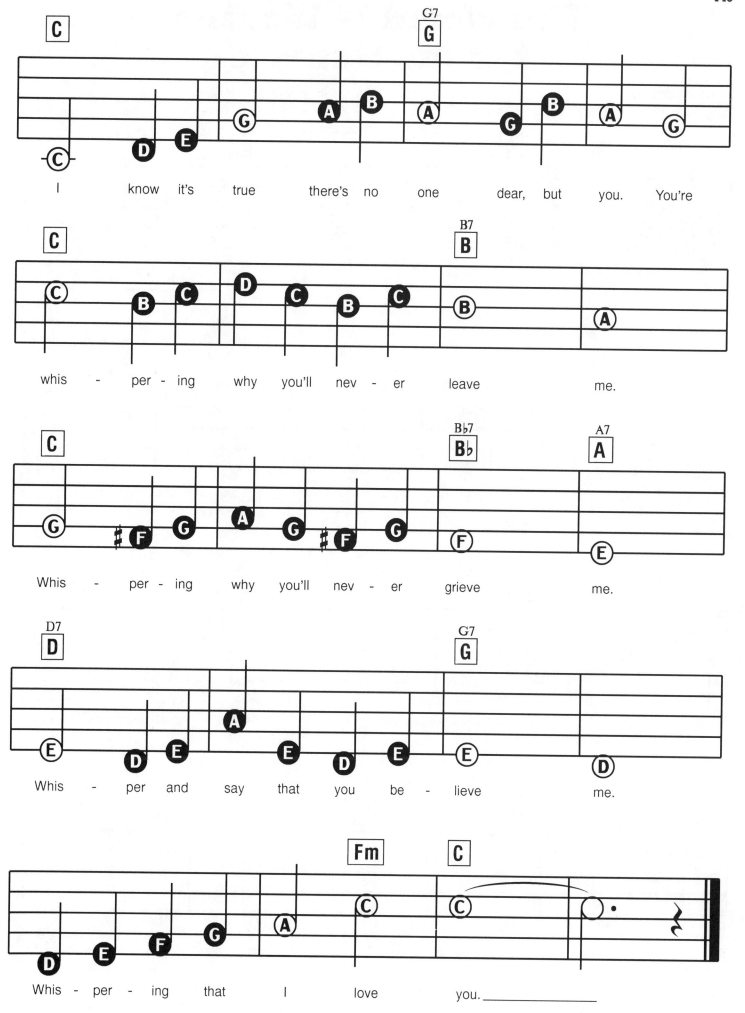

The World Is Waiting for the Sunrise

Registration 5
Rhythm: Fox Trot or Swing

Words by Eugene Lockhart
Music by Ernest Seitz

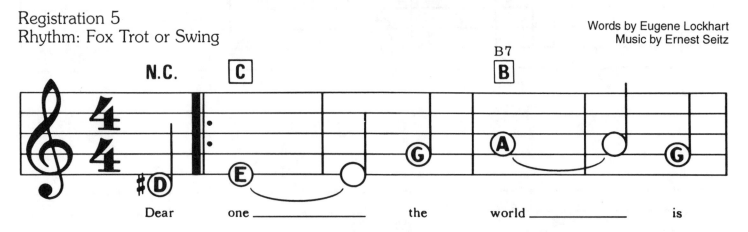

Dear one _____ the world _____ is

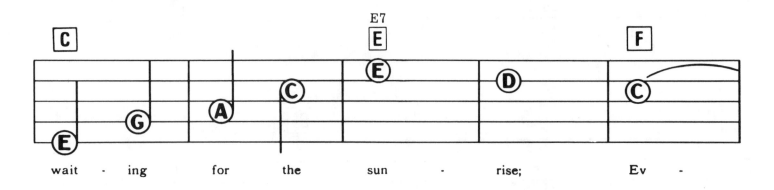

wait - ing for the sun - rise; Ev -

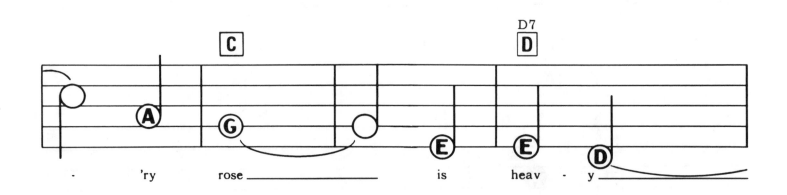

- 'ry rose _____ is heav - y _____

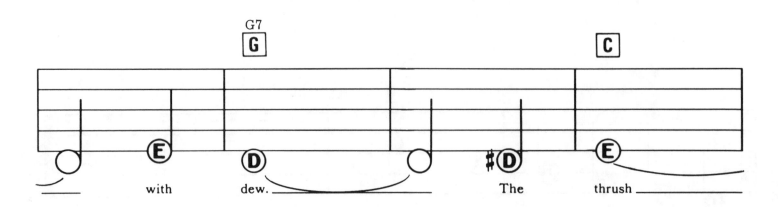

with dew. _____ The thrush _____

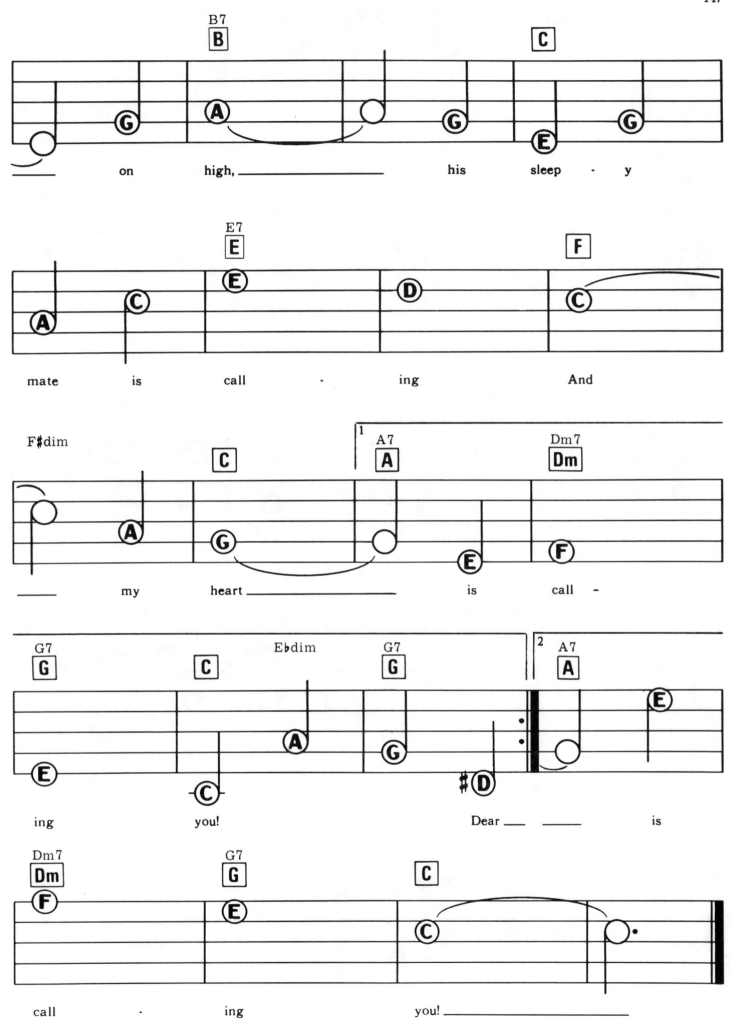

You Made Me Love You
(I Didn't Want to Do It)
from BROADWAY MELODY OF 1938

Registration 7
Rhythm: Fox Trot

Words by Joe McCarthy
Music by James V. Monaco

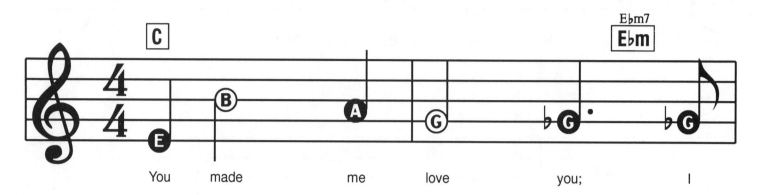

You made me love you; I

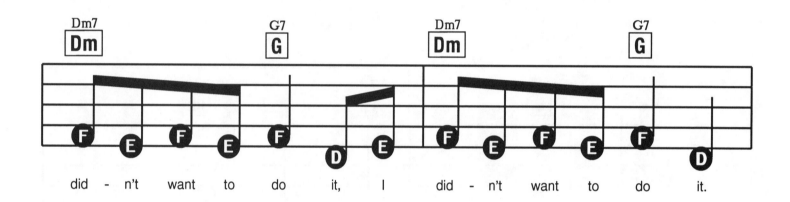

did - n't want to do it, I did - n't want to do it.

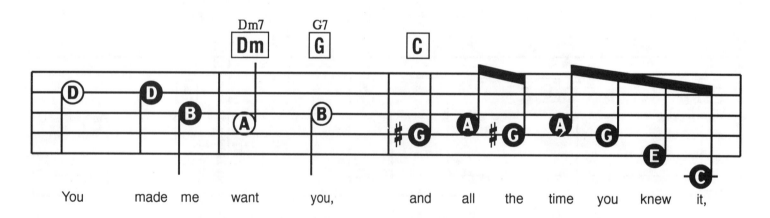

You made me want you, and all the time you knew it,

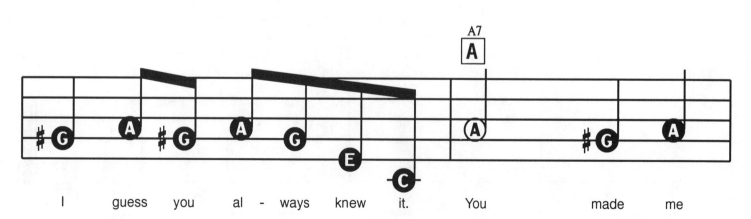

I guess you al - ways knew it. You made me

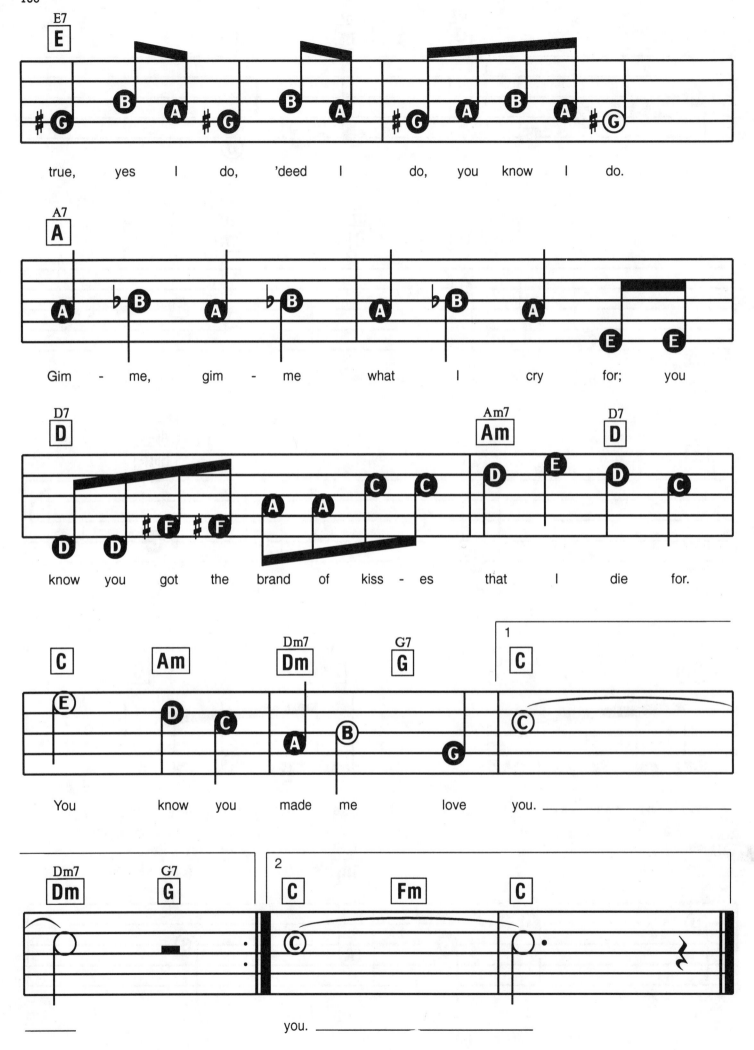